DREAMBOOK + PLANNER

2023

Please visit **dreambook.vision** and
dreambookapp.com for additional resources.

Hang With Us

/thedragontree

@thedragontree

thedragontree.com

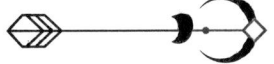 # Table of Contents

Welcome From Our Founders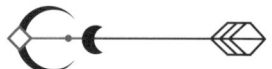

Now is the time to take the first steps toward actualizing your dreams while simultaneously prioritizing your health and happiness. We're so happy to be part of this journey with you, and we firmly believe that if you set out to achieve your goals while remaining steadfast on the necessity of playing, caring for yourself, connecting to family, friends, a higher power, and the natural world – you actually amplify your ability to succeed.

We believe in you and we're honored to help in getting your genius out into the world.

Love,

Briana & Peter

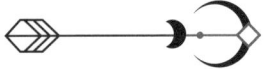 Ritual Makes the Difference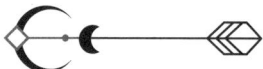

Want to live a meaningful life?

Many of us want to feel a greater sense of meaning and purpose in our lives, but aren't sure where this would come from. The secret is that *we* are in charge of creating the meaning and purpose.

Historically, we had rituals for everything that mattered. But ritual is gradually disappearing as people find they're too busy for it or can't see the value in it. Even a ritual as simple as enjoying the peace of the new morning is so often sacrificed for whatever new alerts our phone might have for us. There's more depression and anxiety than ever before, more uncertainty about where we fit in, and yet, the opportunity to reconnect is always available.

Ritual brings order, specialness, context and focus to our lives. The opening and closing, or the initiation and conclusion of a ritual aligns our intention with our actions, and it sets the stage for the action to be as effective as possible. Ritual grounds us in the present; it rescues us from dwelling on the past and worrying about the future.

You probably already have some rituals – like brewing a cup of coffee and sitting down to plan your day. We believe it's worth bringing more awareness to these rituals, and consciously forging new ones, even if their value is entirely subjective. Your experience of your day and your life will have a structure and specialness that's meaningful to *you*. Wouldn't it be worth it?

You *will* see objective change, too. As you implement healthy rituals, your outlook will change, your beliefs may change, and the world you create around yourself will change. Don't just dream and set goals, ritualize their actualization.

 How This Book Works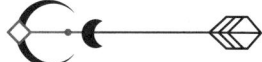

CONNECT

We start by connecting with what's really important to you. This section is designed to help you identify your core values, your gifts, and your life purpose.

DREAM

This is the space to stretch your imagination around what you might think is possible. Stop playing small and start seeing yourself as the magical creator you are. You can create anything you want. We want to help ensure that what you're creating reflects your highest potential and most authentic self.

CRAFT

This is where it gets real. You'll be selecting items from the Dream section to pursue, and you'll create mind maps to flesh them out.

RITUALIZE

Next, it's time to come up with the rituals that will make this process fun, meaningful, and an integral part of your life.

PLAN

Yearly, quarterly, monthly, and weekly planning is essential to keep you on track with your big dreams, your happiness, and your health.

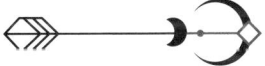 Create Space for
What's Most Important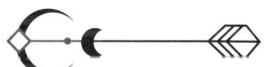

Why the arrows? The arrow theme is a reminder of the incredible power of your attention. It's easy to get distracted from what's important by what feels urgent in the moment, by every new email, or by a list of mundane tasks that "need" our immediate attention. But we encourage you to treat your attention as a valuable thing – like golden arrows – because your energy flows in the direction of your attention. What you put your attention on grows and becomes a theme of your life – whether you mean for this or not.

We invite you to experience a new way of life where YOU are in charge, and you focus your precious energy on what truly matters to you. It's unlikely that anyone gets to the end of life and wishes they had spent more time playing on their phone. As you take your last breaths, what do you want to have done with your life? In the end, only you get to decide if it was a life well lived. You're shaping it right now. If you don't like where you're headed, there's no time like the present to begin changing your course.

With that, we have one big rule for planning:

Schedule what's most important first. Always.

Connect

Consider These Six Main Areas of Life

»—→ Physical Wellness
»—→ Psychological and Spiritual Health
»—→ Creation, Exploration, and Play
»—→ Community Connection
»—→ Livelihood, Career, and Influence
»—→ Relationship and Family

Questions to Connect You to Your True Desires and Purpose

Answer these questions honestly. As if no one else will ever see your answers. As if your parents would be thrilled no matter who you are, no matter what you do with your life. As if no one else's opinion matters. These responses are for you alone, so you have everything to gain by reaching deep.

1. What are you longing for most in life?

_____

_____

_____

_____

_____

2. When you're at the end of life what do you want to have accomplished?

_____

_____

_____

_____

3. If you knew you had one year left to live, would there be anything you'd want to fix or clean up?

_____

_____

4. What are you ready to let go of – habits, attitudes, obligations, beliefs, outdated goals, etc. – that is not serving you?

_____

_____

_____

_____

5. What do you want to explore more deeply?

_____

_____

6. What would make life feel ridiculously fun?

_____

_____

7. What feels really nourishing in your life?

_____

_____

_____

8. Of all the things you've done or accomplished in your life, what has given you the deepest sense of fulfillment? When have you been most proud of yourself?

_____

_____

_____

9. Where do you find yourself not being fully "present" in your life, or not participating fully?

_____

_____

_____

 ## Discovering Your Core Values and Gifts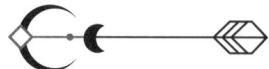

Are you ever faced with a major (or not-so-major) life decision you're uncertain about? Like what to do about a job offer, or a prospective relationship, or a new place to live? We've been there. And we've found that besides a good ol' pros and cons list, it's helpful to have identified your core values. You can reflect on your list to guide you to healthy long term decisions.

For help discovering these values, first look at the answers to your questions in the previous section. Consider your greatest accomplishments and failures. When have you been most productive? When do you like yourself the most? What advice would you give someone based on what you've learned? Look for common themes.

Here are some potential core values to give you ideas from which you can develop and refine your own:

Honesty	Enjoyment	Achievement
Kindness	Flexibility	Lightness
Integrity	Trustworthiness	Learning
Purpose	Beauty	Discipline
Compassion	Courage	Generosity
Love	Wisdom	Devotion
Ambition	Openness	Optimism
Expression	Humility	Respectfulness
Individuality	Simplicity	Vision
Community	Equality	Truthfulness
Service	Righteousness	Persistence

Choose a few values that resonate with you, and follow naturally from your previous answers:

_____

_____

_____

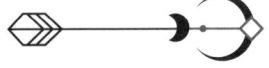 ## Your Gifts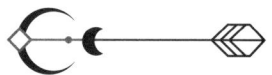

Now, looking again through your previous answers and free writing, what are your talents and gifts? Are you good at helping others to feel heard? Do you have an ability to create art? Are you a gifted communicator? Are you skilled at connecting with children or animals? This is not the time for modesty. Everyone has gifts. Everyone is a healer. Everyone has the capacity to create beauty. Write about your talents and gifts here:

_____

_____

_____

_____

 Purpose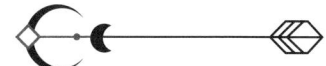

Considering your core values and your gifts, what might your life purpose be? "Life purpose" can sound so grand, so out of our hands. Few people have the experience of knowing their purpose and accessing the clarity that comes from it, because we believe it's a revelation that's delivered through some dramatic or mystical experience. Or that sometimes we're just lucky enough to stumble upon a path that we feel a profound sense of conviction about.

The crazy thing is, rather than waiting around to see if we'll be assigned a life purpose, we can just choose one. If you choose with your heart, you'll choose something that's at least in the right direction, and over time you'll refine and evolve it. Don't worry about getting it perfect.

Frame your purpose as a way that you can serve or help. That is, given your values and gifts, how might these be of value to your species? Or to the planet? Or to children? Or to refugees? Or to endangered plants and animals? Or to any other group that could benefit from your unique talents?

Consider how you could work your core values and gifts into a service-oriented statement of purpose. Such as, "My purpose is to help children heal through art." Or, "My purpose is to empower women to learn and use their voices." Or, "My purpose is to help my species survive through communication." Or, "My purpose is to make the world more beautiful." We'll get you started:

My purpose is _____

Now that you have a clearer sense of your core values, your gifts, and your purpose, it should be easier to get a sense of your priorities. Knowing these "soul drives" can be a valuable guide through difficult experiences and tough decisions.

You can always ask yourself:

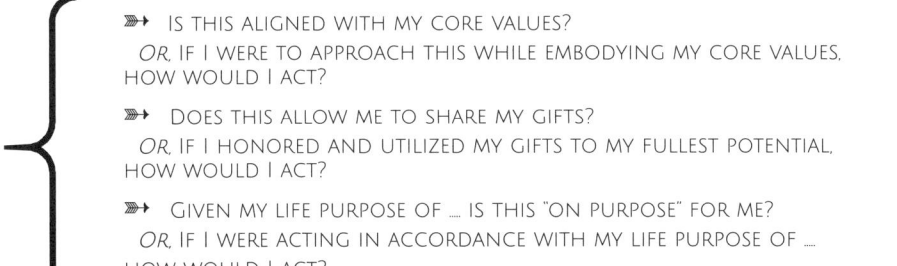

> ≫→ IS THIS ALIGNED WITH MY CORE VALUES?
> OR, IF I WERE TO APPROACH THIS WHILE EMBODYING MY CORE VALUES, HOW WOULD I ACT?
>
> ≫→ DOES THIS ALLOW ME TO SHARE MY GIFTS?
> OR, IF I HONORED AND UTILIZED MY GIFTS TO MY FULLEST POTENTIAL, HOW WOULD I ACT?
>
> ≫→ GIVEN MY LIFE PURPOSE OF ..... IS THIS "ON PURPOSE" FOR ME?
> OR, IF I WERE ACTING IN ACCORDANCE WITH MY LIFE PURPOSE OF ..... HOW WOULD I ACT?

Often, this quickly brings you clarity. You may not be successful at always staying aware and reverent of your values, gifts, and purpose. But when you begin to consciously do this more and more, you'll experience a sense of *alignment* – a *knowing* that you're on the right track – and there's both peace and power in this.

 Evaluate Your Self-Trust

If your plans don't often work out, it will be valuable to look at their underlying *structure* - your agreements. When w make agreements with others, most of us understand the consequences of breaking those agreements. But we're ofte less aware of the impact of breaking agreements with ourselves.

If you serially break agreements with yourself - you don't get things done when you say you'll get them done, you don follow through on the healthy eating habits you resolve to keep, you don't communicate in the way you agreed to, etc. the consequences can be more detrimental than you realize. Your integrity is at stake. As small as they may seem, a lon history of broken agreements equates to an inability to trust yourself. It's also like repeatedly giving yourself the commu nication, "You don't matter," or, "I don't respect you." It can really hurt your relationship with yourself, especially whe it causes you to give up on your dreams.

This book is a perfect challenge in self-trust, because it will only work for you if you do what you say you're going to do But if you do this, you'll discover a certain power and momentum that emanates from your integrity. You empower you word. Everything you say is going to happen, happens. And when you decide to aim for something ambitious, instead o your mind coming up with a bunch of evidence why it's not likely to succeed, you'll feel a sense of conviction that yo can count on yourself - and the Universe knows how to support you!

Re-establishing self-trust is key if you plan to make new agreements that everyone can rely on. Here are four ways t approach that process:

- ⟫→ Be Clear When Defining an Agreement
- ⟫→ Communicate Any Changes in the Agreement
- ⟫→ Clean Up Broken Agreements
- ⟫→ Don't Make Too Many Agreements

When re-establishing self-trust, start with baby steps. You might want to begin with agreements about things you' probably do anyway - so you can ensure your success. Over time, you can add a bit more to your list. But never mak an agreement you think you're likely to break. Eventually, you'll have an impressive dossier on your trustworthines Consider the questions below. They will give you an understanding of how much self-trust you have now. We will re-visi these questions every quarter, so you can track your self-trust, and build even stronger awareness of your agreement with yourself and others.

Self-Trust Personal Assessment: Rate your ability to trust yourself in each of the following areas of life on a scale of 0 to 1(

(Total lack of trust ⓪ ⋯⋯⋯ ⑩ Complete trust)

COMMUNICATION: How much do you trust yourself to tell the truth, say what needs to be said for healthy relationships, speak kindly, and express yourself authentically? _____

DEPENDABILITY: How much do you trust yourself to show up for friends and family, and support them when they need it? _____

TIME MANAGEMENT: How much do you trust yourself to be on time, to stick to your schedule and to plan appropriately? _____

FOLLOW THROUGH: How much do you trust yourself to follow through on your projects, in the time frame intended, to completion? _____

FOCUS: How much do you trust yourself to stay focused on what you have chosen to work on and avoid indulging in distraction? _____

MONEY: How much do you trust yourself to stay conscious of what you have, to maintain a positive attitude around money and to avoid taking on unnecessary debt? _____

HEALTH MAINTENANCE: How much do you trust yourself to treat your body and soul well, to get the care you need and to be kind to yourself? _____

NUTRITION: How much do you trust yourself to make good food choices, to eat in a healthy manner and to stick with your agreements around eating? _____

WORK PERFORMANCE: How much do you trust yourself to honor the work you do, to do your best and to show up enthusiastically? _____

VALUES: How much do you trust yourself to live by your core values? _____

 Visualize

Take a minute to close your eyes and imagine your ideal life three years in the future. Everything has worked out in your favor. Really feel what's aroused in you when you know you'll be happy and peaceful, and tune into how you experience this in your heart. Then open your eyes and draw something here that emanates from this feeling. Imagine there's an energetic circuit connecting your heart to your hand, and just draw. It could be a picture of this future you, or your future life, or it could be something more abstract. Don't put a lot of thought into it, but do put a lot of heart into it.

Dream

Imagine your life three years from now, and create a positive picture using the questions below. Really feel into exactly what you want. You can have anything - you just have to choose.

 ## Livelihood, Career, Influence

Projecting three years into the future of your wildest dreams, consider these details about how you earn money, the work you do, and the nature of your influence on the world. Answer all the questions from this perspective.

1. What does your business/career look and feel like?

_____

_____

_____

2. How much money do you make? What other benefits do you get?

_____

_____

3. How do you feel when you get up in the morning to start your work day (even if this work isn't how you earn money)?

_____

_____

_____

4. What do people say about what you do? How is your reputation?

_____

_____

_____

Remember to answer these questions from the perspective of your ideal future.

5. Who / what kinds of people do you work with?

_____

_____

_____

6. What is your ultimate vision for the financial life you're headed toward (income, investments, savings, etc.)?

_____

_____

_____

_____

7. What sort of influence do you have on your community? What value do you bring to the world?

_____

_____

_____

_____

_____

8. How do you feel about paying bills, taxes, or unforeseen expenses?

_____

_____

_____

9. How do you feel when you check your bank account?

_____

_____

_____

10. How do you spend your money in ways that make you feel you're having a positive impact?

_____

_____

_____

 Relationship and Family

Projecting three years into the future of your happiest dreams, consider these details about how you want your love relationship and family life to be. Answer all the questions from this perspective – as if you have already attained this.

1. Describe your primary love relationship.

_____

_____

_____

_____

2. In this ideal relationship, what do you give, receive, create, and experience together? Consider all the realms of your relationship, including love, intimacy, friendship, support, play, etc.

_____

_____

_____

_____

3. How do you feel when you're talking with your partner? When you're expressing something that matters to you, or makes you feel vulnerable?

_____

_____

_____

_____

4. How do you grow through being in this relationship?

_____

_____

_____

_____

Remember to answer these questions from the perspective of your ideal future.

5. In your ideal family life, how does it feel when everyone is home together?

_____

_____

_____

_____

6. What do you and your family members do together?

_____

_____

_____

_____

7. What are family conversations like? How does your family respond when you speak from your heart about something that is very important to you?

_____

_____

_____

_____

8. How does the family respond if someone has a problem?

_____

_____

_____

_____

9. What are holidays like together?

_____

_____

_____

_____

 Community Connection

Projecting three years into the future of your most delighted dreams, consider these details about how you want your community to be. Answer all the questions from this perspective – as if you have already attained this.

1. What are your friendships like? What do you do together?

_____

_____

_____

_____

_____

2. How prominently do your friends figure into your everyday life? How often do you get together?

_____

_____

_____

_____

3. How are your conversations? Are you able to share on all matters that concern you?

_____

_____

_____

_____

4. How do your friends respond when you're having a difficult time?

_____

_____

_____

_____

_____

Remember to answer these questions from the perspective of your ideal future.

5. How do you and your friends support each other?

_____

_____

_____

6. What needs of yours are met by your friendships?

_____

_____

_____

7. Describe your community:

_____

_____

_____

_____

8. How do you engage with your community? In what way do you fit in?

_____

_____

_____

9. How are you nourished and/or supported by your community?

_____

_____

_____

10. What value do you bring to your community?

_____

_____

_____

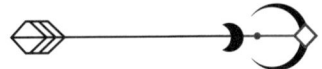 Physical Wellness

Projecting three years into the future of your most healthy and vibrant dreams, consider these details about how you want your body, energy, and overall health to be. Answer all the questions from this perspective – as if you have already attained this.

1. Describe your beautiful body.

_____

_____

_____

_____

2. How do you feel in your body when you wake up in the morning?

_____

_____

3. How do you feel in your body at the end of a long day?

_____

_____

4. How is your relationship with exercise, and what do you do to keep your body in good shape?

_____

_____

_____

_____

5. How do you feed your body? What do you eat, and *how* do you eat?

_____

_____

_____

_____

Remember to answer these questions from the perspective of your ideal future.

6. How is your energy?

_____

_____

_____

7. How is your sleep?

_____

_____

_____

8. How does it feel when you take a deep breath?

_____

_____

_____

9. How are your strength and flexibility?

_____

_____

_____

10. How do you feel about aging?

_____

_____

_____

11. If you used to have any health problems, what has happened with these?

_____

_____

_____

_____

 Creation, Exploration and Play

Projecting three years into the future of your most fun and fascinating dreams, consider these details about how you want to be engaging and expressing yourself creatively, intellectually, and playfully. Answer all the questions from this perspective – as if you have already attained this.

1. What percentage of your life is reserved for playing, exploring, and creating?

_____

2. How much do you travel, and to where?

_____

_____

_____

3. What forms of creative expression do you engage in (painting, drawing, sculpting, gardening, singing, playing an instrument, writing, acting, photography, dancing, building, sewing, etc.)?

_____

_____

_____

_____

4. How is your life affected by prioritizing creative expression, exploration, and play?

_____

_____

_____

_____

5. What forms of play and exploration do you engage in, and how often?

_____

_____

_____

Remember to answer these questions from the perspective of your ideal future.

6. Who else do you involve in your creative and playful endeavors, and what role do they play?

7. Do you have a space just for doing your creative thing? What's it like?

8. What forums do you have for exploring the topics you're passionate about with others?

9. What fascinates you?

10. In what ways is your life beautiful, and how do you live it in a beautiful way?

 ## Psychological and Spiritual Health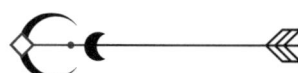

Projecting three years into the future of your most lucid and uplifting dreams, consider these details about how you want to be thinking, feeling, and connecting. Answer all the questions from this perspective – as if you have already attained this.

1. What percentage of your waking life do you feel happy?

_____

2. Describe your outlook on life, and the quality of your thoughts:

_____

_____

_____

_____

3. What percentage of your communications come from a place of truth and love? And how does this affect you and others in your life?

_____

_____

_____

4. How do you feel and respond during challenging times?

_____

_____

_____

5. Do you trust yourself to manage whatever might happen?

_____

_____

6. What percentage of your life is spent in a peaceful state?

_____

Remember to answer these questions from the perspective of your ideal future.

7. In what ways do you express love to others, the world, and your higher power?

_____

_____

8. How is your life affected by your cultivating a more peaceful and loving experience?

_____

_____

9. How do you connect to your Higher Self, God, or The Universe? What does it feel like?

_____

_____

_____

10. How do you feel about the state of the world, and your place in it?

_____

_____

_____

11. How is your self-esteem?

_____

_____

12. How do you feel about the new day when you wake up in the morning?

_____

_____

13. How do you feel about dying?

_____

_____

_____

_____

Craft

Now, a message to you from your Highest Self:

Thank you for taking the time to let me express myself and make my deepest wishes known. I am absolutely ready to step into the reality you just wrote about. I know we can do it together! You might want to let me steer more often, though. I love you.

The material you came up with was not just a psychological exercise, but a window to your true dreams. Use your answers to determine the qualities and behaviors you plan to cultivate from this day forward.

Now it's time to start crafting the tangible goals that align with your unique truth, gifts, and purpose. A mind map is a visual representation of ideas that makes it easy to organize concepts and connections. On the following pages, you are going to create maps of the goals you will achieve in the next year, in 3 years, in 10 years, and over your lifetime. Frame all goals in the positive – i.e., what you want to have, be, or do – not what you want to avoid or get rid of. Consider all the areas of your life we went through in the previous section: physical wellness; psychological and spiritual health; creation, exploration, and play; community connection; livelihood, career and influence; relationship and family. Here is an example:

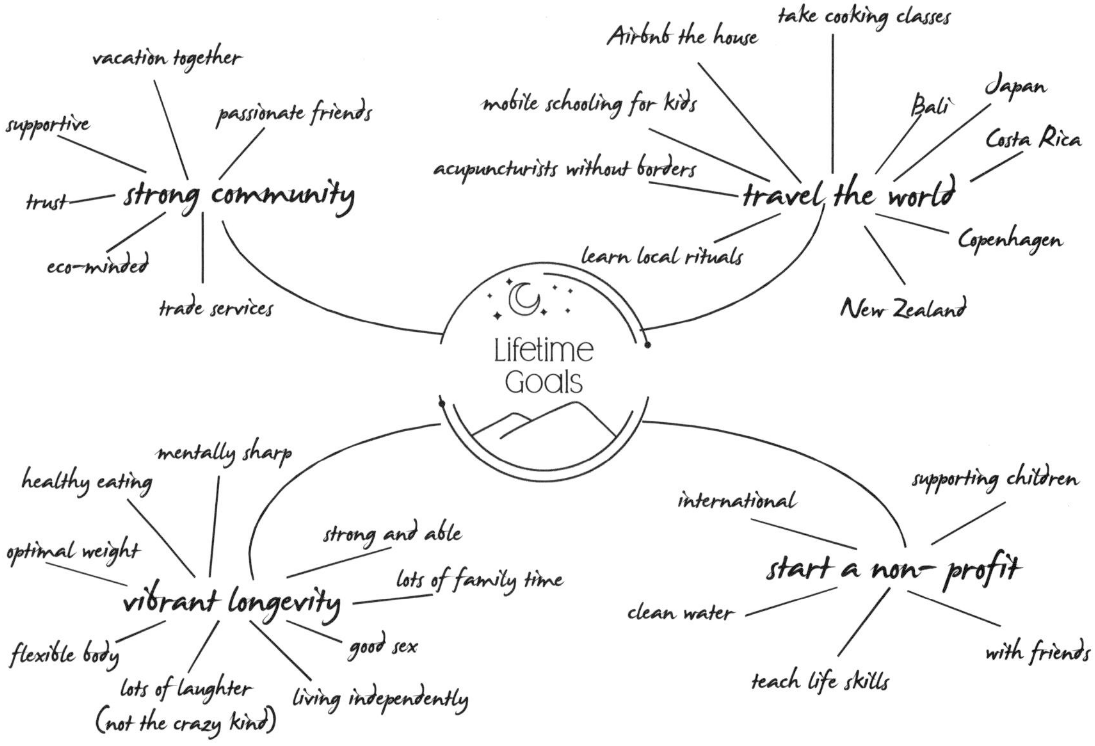

take cooking classes

Airbnb the house

mobile schooling for kids

vacation together

passionate friends

supportive

acupuncturists without borders

Bali

Japan

Costa Rica

trust — **strong community**

travel the world

eco-minded

learn local rituals

Copenhagen

trade services

New Zealand

Lifetime Goals

mentally sharp

healthy eating

strong and able

international

supporting children

optimal weight

lots of family time

start a non-profit

vibrant longevity

clean water

flexible body

good sex

with friends

lots of laughter
(not the crazy kind)

living independently

teach life skills

1 Year

3 Years

Lifetime

 Break it Down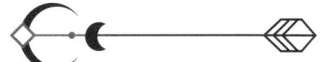

Simply recognizing how important these goals are to us doesn't necessarily ensure that we'll start knocking them out, meditating, eating better, and healing our relationship with our parents. We say this not to discourage you, but to explain that most people need more structure, more hand-holding, and more ritual in order to make this stuff stick.

That's why we'll immediately proceed to selecting goals, breaking these goals down into projects, breaking the projects down into actionable steps, getting these actions into your calendar, and forging rituals to stabilize your new paradigm.

Choose three goals from each mind map (life, 10 years, 3 years, and 1 year). Ask yourself, *why is* **this** *goal important to me?* When you've selected three, map each one with projects necessary to achieve this goal. Most of these projects will involve multiple actions, though some may be single actionable steps.

If you have a hard time considering how to reach a goal, start from the end result and work backwards. What would have to happen right before you reach your goal? And what would have to happen right before that? And right before that?

For each project, include your expected date of completion. These dates should be realistic, neither too loose nor too demanding. Set yourself up to succeed. Here's an example:

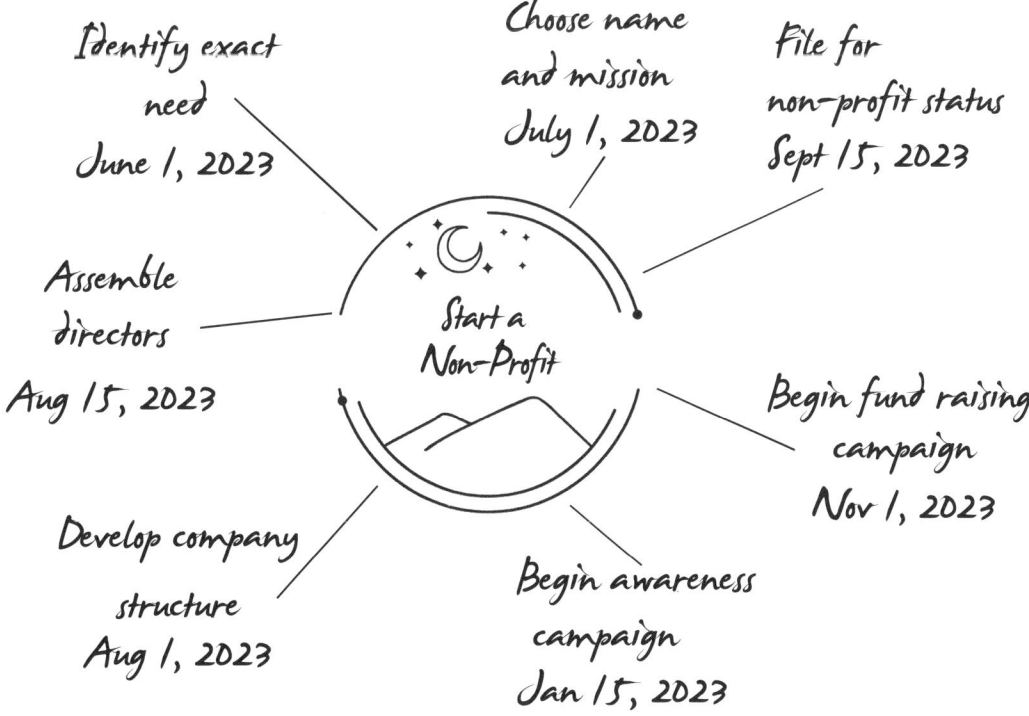

Identify exact need
June 1, 2023

Choose name and mission
July 1, 2023

File for non-profit status
Sept 15, 2023

Assemble directors
Aug 15, 2023

Start a Non-Profit

Begin fund raising campaign
Nov 1, 2023

Develop company structure
Aug 1, 2023

Begin awareness campaign
Jan 15, 2023

One Year Goals

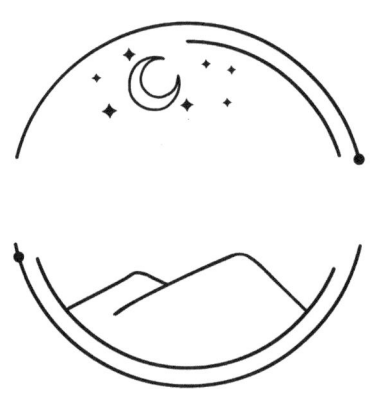

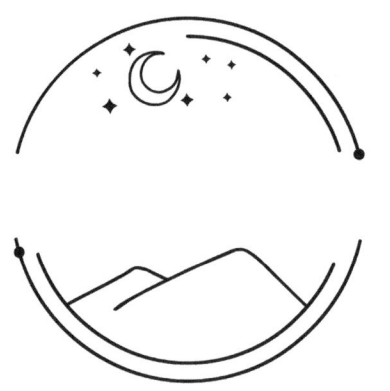

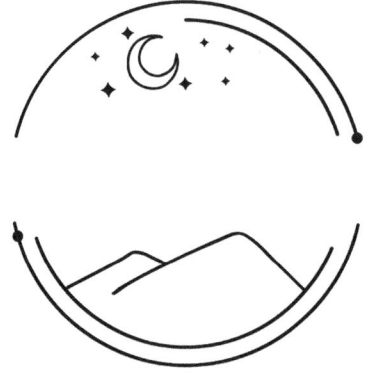

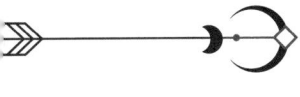

28

Three Year Goals

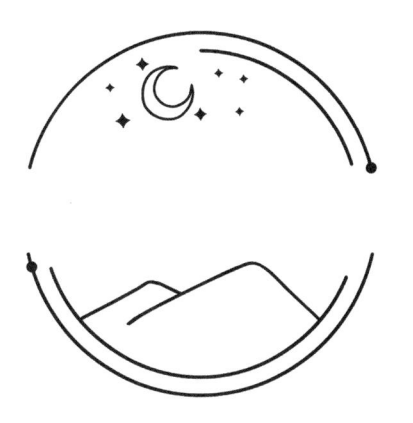

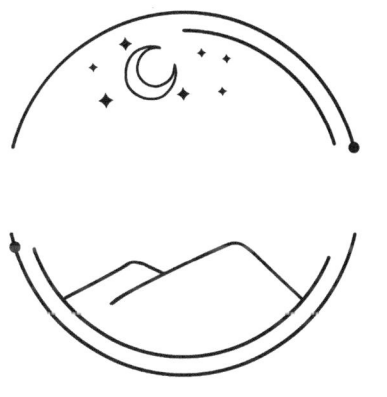

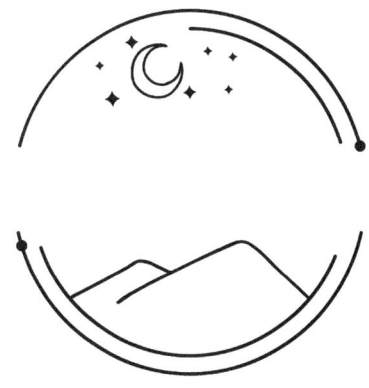

Ten Year Goals

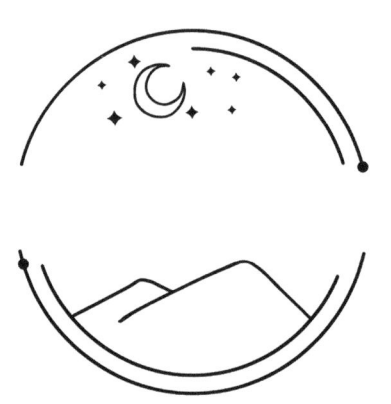

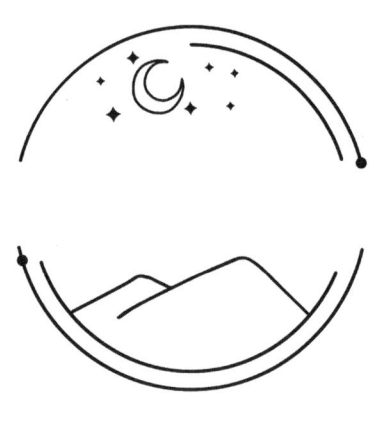

Lifetime Goals

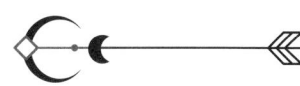

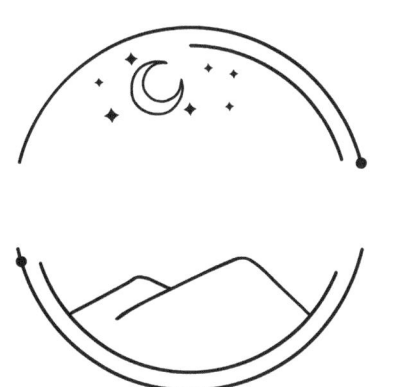

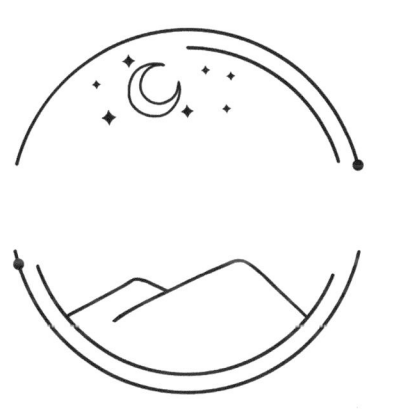

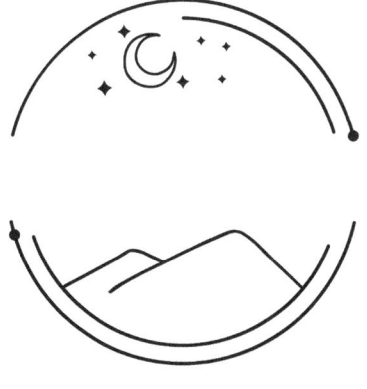

Ritualize

We've finally come to the Ritual part of Rituals for Living. This is where you get to make life more special for yourself. Many of us have an aversion to ritual because it seems to add extra time and energy to what we want to get done fast. If this is the case for you, we encourage you to ask yourself, *Where am I trying to get to so fast that I'm willing to sacrifice savoring the present?* It might also be worth considering whether the rituals around you, or the ones you've adopted from your family or community, aren't *yours*. If so, make up new ones that are meaningful and enjoyable for you. You'll never regret making the time for this.

Our top priority is to help you create a ritual around planning, but we encourage you to develop rituals around:

1. Any practice that you want to become more of a fixture in your life, such as exercise or cooking

2. Any everyday act that you want to enhance the specialness of, such as mealtimes or bathing

3. Any act that you want to transform into a grounding or tuning-in point in your life

As for planning, once a year simply isn't enough. In order to accomplish big things while maintaining a clean mental space, planning must become an integral part of your life. There's no reason to dread it – it can be enjoyable, and can actually help you feel lighter. As soon as events change, and the plan we've been working from needs modification, we feel a certain sense of unease until we check in and update the plan. It might be a very subtle feeling that's easy to ignore, but when we have major plans, the unease can feel quite strong. If something feels off, check in with your plan: Is something out of sync? Have you broken an agreement? Do you have a need that isn't being met? Revise the plan and/or your attitude. Clarity always feels good.

A ritual doesn't need to be ceremonious, but consider this: the more special you make your rituals, the more specialness there will be in your life. It's almost too simplistic to take it seriously, but it's true in so many areas of life, so we encourage you to let that sink in for a moment.

The most fundamental requirement of a ritual is that you're *deliberate* about it. This might mean that you tune in, take a single breath, and express to yourself what you intend to do. When you're done, you tune in, take a breath, and express that you have gratefully concluded the ritual. This could take literally ten seconds.

But adding additional elements that you're consistent about can make your rituals something you look forward to; it can make help cement your rituals more firmly into your life; and it can make it easier to quickly "drop in" to an efficient, lucid, or inspired state.

Consider the following elements for ideas. Think of them as ways to "bookend" your ritual, to set it apart from the everyday, and to lend greater potency to what you set out to do. These elements have set the stage for some of our most powerful planning and ideation sessions, our most efficient work, and our deepest meditations.

 Elements of Ritual

Fire: A candle, a fireplace, an oil lamp, or the sun. Fire is a symbol of illumination, warmth, and connection.
Words: Set an intention, say a blessing or mantra, invoke a helper. Writing can make words even more "real."
Food or Drink: Consuming food/drink is special as it involves bringing something from the outside world into your body. Plus, it incorporates the senses of taste and smell, and may produce a biological response.
Beauty: Adorning and beautifying your space, your things, and your life is a way of elevating them beyond the mundane, and of demonstrating gratitude & reverence.
Sound: Trickling water, bells, chimes, chants, binaural beats, and favorite songs can all help tune our attention.
Garments: Putting on a special necklace, shawl, hat or superhero outfit may help you get into the right space.
Water: Water symbolizes purity, cleansing, and flow. Bathe, dip your hands in it, or splash some on your face.
Scents: Flowers, incense, and essential oils have long been used to uplift our consciousness and shift the space around us to designate a special purpose.
Gathering: Strength in numbers. Whether co-working or co-ritualizing, tuning in together can be stronger.
Location: The woods, the beach, or your altar in the bathroom. A consistent space can help focus your ritual.
Objects of Significance: A cup, a crystal, a lock of Bon Jovi's hair – these can help anchor you in your ritual.
Timing: Synchronizing a ritual with a particular season, the birthday of someone important, a historic event, a moon phase, time of day, the solstice, equinox, etc., may contribute to a sense of extra power and alignment.

Answer these questions to reveal factors that will be most natural for you to integrate into your rituals:

1. When and where do you feel you're most inspired and focused?

_____

2. What clothing makes you feel most in your element? Sweats? Black tie? Kippa? Mala? Lucky socks?

_____

3. What's your favorite food or drink to consume while pondering your future and accessing your inner strength?

_____

4. Do you have any treasured objects that make you feel inspired or uplifted? Photo? Feather?

_____

5. What helps you feel centered and grounded? Turning off your cell phone? Taking a bath? Running a mile?

_____

6. Are there any sounds or scents that help you relax or put you in a transcendent space?

_____

7. Which of the elements in the list above do you feel a natural attraction to?

_____

_____

Plan

 What I Will Accomplish This Year

1. Get into your *ritual for planning* space. Do your thing (light a candle, take a breath, go to a peaceful spot, set an intention, etc.).

2. Flip back to the mind maps you created for the three goals you selected for the next one year, three years, ten years, and your lifetime. Mark any projects that will be *beginning or continuing* in the coming year. Enter these projects in the table below, and mark the appropriate number(s) for the quarter(s) in which the project will take place.

Project	Quarter			
Example: *find a book agent*	①	●	③	④
	①	②	③	④
	①	②	③	④
	①	②	③	④
	①	②	③	④
	①	②	③	④
	①	②	③	④
	①	②	③	④
	①	②	③	④
	①	②	③	④
	①	②	③	④
	①	②	③	④
	①	②	③	④
	①	②	③	④

Project	Quarter			
	①	②	③	④
	①	②	③	④
	①	②	③	④
	①	②	③	④
	①	②	③	④
	①	②	③	④
	①	②	③	④
	①	②	③	④
	①	②	③	④
	①	②	③	④
	①	②	③	④
	①	②	③	④
	①	②	③	④
	①	②	③	④
	①	②	③	④
	①	②	③	④
	①	②	③	④
	①	②	③	④

 Theme of the Year

Set an intention for the coming year by giving it a theme. It's a good way to designate an overarching focus, and you may be surprised at how the experiences of the year fit the theme you choose. You can write your theme in the space below, and phrase it as such: "The Year of Learning to Love Myself" or "The Year of Forgiveness" or "The Year of Letting Go of the Struggle" or "The Year of Coming into My Power." Feel free to get artistic in how you write this. Go!

 How to Work Your Plan

Please read these directions. They're *essential* for getting the most out of your Dreambook – and they'll make the process feel less daunting.

1. Schedule your projects for the current quarter.

Each quarter begins with a **Quarterly Breakdown**. Turn one page back to the projects you wrote down on the **Plan** pages (AKA "What I Will Accomplish This Year"), identify which ones will happen in the current quarter (plus any unfinished projects from the last quarter) and write them all down in the column labeled **Project** on the **Quarterly Breakdown** page.

For each project, decide which of the three months of the quarter you'll be working on it. Then mark or fill in one or more of the circles corresponding to the appropriate month(s).

2. Break down the quarter's projects into tasks.

There is a **Project Breakdown** page for each month in the quarter. Go through the **Quarterly Breakdown** you just completed. For each project, go to the **Project Breakdown** page for the month(s) in which it will be happening, and copy the project name onto one of the lines labeled **Project.**

Under each Project line, write down all the tasks involved in that project. Make sure these are actionable tasks, meaning each one can be started without any further breakdown necessary. These tasks will later be scheduled into your daily planner (or electronic calendar), and we don't want you to lose momentum if you encounter a task that's actually a *project* that involves numerous tasks.

3. Use the **Monthly Calendar** located at the beginning of each month.

You can record events and notes here, to be scheduled more precisely in the daily planner before each week begins.

4. Use the **Weekly Alignment** page to set the tone for each week (before the week begins!)

Everything about the Weekly Alignment and daily planner sections is intended to support you to stay focused on what's most important, to keep aligning yourself with your values, gifts, and purpose, to remember the quality of life and perspective you're choosing, and to support you to grow and emerge as your best self.

Throughout the week, start each day by taking a glance at what you've written on the **Weekly Alignment** page.

⬨ **Top 3 Goals**:

Here you will write three goals you intend to accomplish over the week (these are likely "small goals" compared to the ones you mapped, or might be the sub-projects of your larger goals).

⬨ **Focus Box**:

Here you can write a focus you choose for the week, such as "Be mindful," "Communicate clearly," "Stay positive," "Take frequent breaks," "One day at a time," or "Center myself before meetings."

⬨ **Habit Tracking**:

Use this tool to track your progress in establishing healthy habits or removing unhealthy ones. Write a habit next to each of the symbols (choose up to four). Throughout the week, indicate your success each day with each habit by marking the appropriate symbol (under the gratitude box for that day).

Mark the symbols in a way that's meaningful to you. For instance, if the habit is jogging each day, you may simply put a check mark in the symbol to indicate that you did it, or leave it blank to indicate that you didn't. Your success at certain habits might be better measured on a scale – such as a number from 1 to 10, or a letter grade (A-, C+, D, etc.).

Habits will be harder to establish if they don't align with the kind of person you believe yourself to be. If you align a new habit with your life purpose, values, and identities, it's more likely to "stick" in a permanent way. When considering a new habit, look back at your values and purpose, and ask yourself, "Who would I be if I embodied these qualities and lived this habit?" or "For what kind of person would these qualities and this habit come naturally?" Write down your answer.

For instance, if the desired habit is daily exercise, you might identify underlying core values such as vibrant health, relishing life, living to your potential, and leading by example. This may clarify that who you want to be is a fit and healthy person who loves life. If you see yourself this way, then behaviors that support health and aliveness come naturally.

More important than simply performing a certain behavior (the new habit) is that you become the person who embodies what the habit represents. As you live the habits of this chosen identity, you reinforce that you are the person you aim to be.

⬨ **Rituals for Living Challenge**:

Each week we present a challenge – an adventure that's designed to nourish, expand, or heal your body and/or mind. We encourage you to participate with all your enthusiasm. You won't regret it!

◇ **Rituals for Thriving**:

We put this list in every **Weekly Alignment** because we want to remind you over and over to prioritize the things that most deeply nourish your body, mind, and soul. Choose from our list or come up with your own, and schedule them liberally into your life.

◇ **Three Questions for Healing and Evolution**

We offer these three prompts to encourage you to engage in an ongoing practice of looking inside, noticing what you're struggling with, remembering your ability to choose your perspective, utilizing your purpose and gifts, exercising your creative power, etc.

Wins From Last Week

It's important to acknowledge what's working well in your life. It keeps your attention on the positive, shows you the effect of your intentions, and strengthens your ability to create the life you desire.

How Will I Reframe Something You Find Difficult, Painful, or Stressful?

Perspective is a superpower. When you change your perspective, you change your experience. Although it may seem that a stressful or unpleasant part of your life is entirely bad, the ability to be lighthearted – or at least accepting – is a choice that's always available. Find the opportunity. The more you practice this, the more resilient you become.

How Will I Create More Freedom in Your Life This Week?

While we hope that the Dreambook helps you achieve your goals, we also want you to feel more free. There are lots of ways to cultivate freedom. Here are a few examples: forgive someone, forgive yourself, meditate, take more breaks, breathe deeply, keep actively choosing your perspective, bring your purpose to the conversation, practice mindfulness.

5. Use the **Capture Your Brilliance** pages for extra space.

These blank pages are meant for note-taking, dreaming, expanding, recording, reflecting, or just doodling.

6. Use the **Weekly Planner** to stay on track.

◇ **Tasks:**

Here you will write down the tasks you'll be accomplishing this week. These include:

o Tasks from the **Project Breakdown** pages for this month
o Leftover tasks to clean up from the previous week
o All of your other life duties
o **Rituals for Thriving** you've chosen to enjoy this week

When scheduling the coming week, you'll take everything from this task list and write it into the calendar, with a beginning time *and end* time – this will help keep the task from sprawling.

◈ **Intention**:

Each day features a space to set an intention. Keep it simple. It could even be a single word or short phrase like: Breathe, Be Efficient, Choose Joy, Social Media Fast, Connect, Keep Moving, Love, Be Present, Remember Your Purpose, Eat Healthy, etc.

◈ **Gratitude**:

At the bottom of each day is a little space for writing what you're grateful for. It's a great way to start and/or end the day. Studies show that writing about your gratitude makes people happier. The more you express (and experience) gratitude, the more aware you become of everything there is to be grateful for. It's also a valuable practice for keeping your focus on what you want more of in your life, rather than the common habit of focusing on what you dislike.

7. Honor your word and keep your agreements.

When you write something in your calendar, this forms an agreement with yourself and an intention to actualize what you've chosen. Following through builds momentum and self-trust. It demonstrates respect for your creative power. Knowing you always do what you say you'll do creates an element of certainty in an uncertain world, and it promotes a clear and peaceful mind.

8. Do it with friends and family!

Sharing this process with others makes it more effective. You get to harness the power of group consciousness – even if the group is just you and a friend. Planning with others promotes clarity and alignment. You can offer each other feedback, support, and inspiration. And for those whose lives are intertwined, sharing this process increases the likelihood that your plans will work out in a mutually beneficial and harmonious way.

One of the most valuable ways to support each other is through "accountability partnerships." We use this structure to lovingly and firmly hold each other accountable for what we've said we're going to do. Knowing someone is tracking us – and our integrity is at stake – can be a strong incentive to stick to it. Agree to check in at the end of each day or at key points in your goal achievement process. Keep your check-ins purposeful – don't be too willing to let each other off the hook. Each should ask the other if they've kept all their agreements. If not, what's getting in the way? Figure out how to clean it up and get back on track.

9. Please visit our website.

Go to **www.dreambook.vision** for more details about everything here, answers to your questions, exercises, and valuable resources. And come join our amazing community on Facebook in the Dragontree Community and Conversations group.

2023

JANUARY

Monday	Tuesday	Wednesday	Thursday	Friday	Saturday	Sunday
						1
2	3	4	5	6	7	8
9	10	11	12	13	14	15
16	17	18	19	20	21	22
23 / 30	24 / 31	25	26	27	28	29

FEBRUARY

Monday	Tuesday	Wednesday	Thursday	Friday	Saturday	Sunday
		1	2	3	4	5
6	7	8	9	10	11	12
13	14	15	16	17	18	19
20	21	22	23	24	25	26
27	28					

MAY

Monday	Tuesday	Wednesday	Thursday	Friday	Saturday	Sunday
1	2	3	4	5	6	7
8	9	10	11	12	13	14
15	16	17	18	19	20	21
22	23	24	25	26	27	28
29	30	31				

JUNE

Monday	Tuesday	Wednesday	Thursday	Friday	Saturday	Sunday
			1	2	3	4
5	6	7	8	9	10	11
12	13	14	15	16	17	18
19	20	21	22	23	24	25
26	27	28	29	30		

SEPTEMBER

Monday	Tuesday	Wednesday	Thursday	Friday	Saturday	Sunday
				1	2	3
4	5	6	7	8	9	10
11	12	13	14	15	16	17
18	19	20	21	22	23	24
25	26	27	28	29	30	

OCTOBER

Monday	Tuesday	Wednesday	Thursday	Friday	Saturday	Sunday
						1
2	3	4	5	6	7	8
9	10	11	12	13	14	15
16	17	18	19	20	21	22
23 / 30	24 / 31	25	26	27	28	29

Year at a Glance

MARCH

Monday	Tuesday	Wednesday	Thursday	Friday	Saturday	Sunday
		1	2	3	4	5
6	7	8	9	10	11	12
13	14	15	16	17	18	19
20	21	22	23	24	25	26
27	28	29	30	31		

APRIL

Monday	Tuesday	Wednesday	Thursday	Friday	Saturday	Sunday
				1	2	
3	4	5	6	7	8	9
10	11	12	13	14	15	16
17	18	19	20	21	22	23
24	25	26	27	28	29	30

JULY

Monday	Tuesday	Wednesday	Thursday	Friday	Saturday	Sunday
					1	2
3	4	5	6	7	8	9
10	11	12	13	14	15	16
17	18	19	20	21	22	23
4 / 31	25	26	27	28	29	30

AUGUST

Monday	Tuesday	Wednesday	Thursday	Friday	Saturday	Sunday
	1	2	3	4	5	6
7	8	9	10	11	12	13
14	15	16	17	18	19	20
21	22	23	24	25	26	27
28	29	30	31			

NOVEMBER

Monday	Tuesday	Wednesday	Thursday	Friday	Saturday	Sunday
		1	2	3	4	5
6	7	8	9	10	11	12
13	14	15	16	17	18	19
20	21	22	23	24	25	26
27	28	29	30			

DECEMBER

Monday	Tuesday	Wednesday	Thursday	Friday	Saturday	Sunday
				1	2	3
4	5	6	7	8	9	10
11	12	13	14	15	16	17
18	19	20	21	22	23	24
25	26	27	29	29	30	31

 Quarter One Breakdown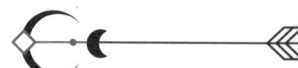

1. Get into your *ritual for planning* space. Do whatever you do to tune in (light a candle, take a breath, go to a peaceful spot, set an intention, etc.).

2. Look back at your What I Will Accomplish This Year list, and find all the projects that will be occurring in the coming quarter. Write each one in the table below and mark the appropriate month number(s) for the month(s) in which it will taking place.

Project	Month		
	Jan	Feb	Mar
	①	②	③
	①	②	③
	①	②	③
	①	②	③
	①	②	③
	①	②	③
	①	②	③
	①	②	③
	①	②	③
	①	②	③
	①	②	③
	①	②	③
	①	②	③
	①	②	③
	①	②	③
	①	②	③
	①	②	③
	①	②	③
	①	②	③
	①	②	③
	①	②	③
	①	②	③
	①	②	③
	①	②	③

Project	Month		
	Jan	Feb	Mar
	①	②	③
	①	②	③
	①	②	③
	①	②	③
	①	②	③
	①	②	③
	①	②	③
	①	②	③
	①	②	③
	①	②	③
	①	②	③
	①	②	③
	①	②	③
	①	②	③
	①	②	③
	①	②	③
	①	②	③
	①	②	③
	①	②	③
	①	②	③
	①	②	③
	①	②	③
	①	②	③
	①	②	③
	①	②	③
	①	②	③
	①	②	③
	①	②	③
	①	②	③
	①	②	③
	①	②	③
	①	②	③
	①	②	③

 January
Project Breakdown

1. Get into your *ritual for planning* space.

2. Gather the projects from the Quarterly Breakdown that pertain to this month and write each one on a PROJECT line below.

3. Under the project name, enter all of the tasks that are involved in the project. Each of these tasks must be a single action step so that it can be put into your calendar and when you see it, no analysis needs to occur – you know exactly what to do.

_____
PROJECT

_____   _____

_____   _____

_____   _____

_____   _____

_____   _____

_____   _____

_____   _____

_____
PROJECT

_____   _____

_____   _____

_____   _____

_____   _____

_____   _____

_____   _____

_____   _____

PROJECT

_____   _____
_____   _____
_____   _____
_____   _____
_____   _____
_____   _____
_____   _____

PROJECT

_____   _____
_____   _____
_____   _____
_____   _____
_____   _____
_____   _____
_____   _____

PROJECT

_____   _____
_____   _____
_____   _____
_____   _____
_____   _____
_____   _____
_____   _____

February
Project Breakdown

1. Get into your *ritual for planning* space.

2. Gather the projects from the Quarterly Breakdown that pertain to this month and write each one on a PROJECT line below.

3. Under the project name, enter all of the tasks that are involved in the project. Each of these tasks must be a single action step so that it can be put into your calendar and when you see it, no analysis needs to occur – you know exactly what to do.

PROJECT

_____   _____

_____   _____

_____   _____

_____   _____

_____   _____

_____   _____

_____   _____

PROJECT

_____   _____

_____   _____

_____   _____

_____   _____

_____   _____

_____   _____

_____   _____

PROJECT

_____   _____
_____   _____
_____   _____
_____   _____
_____   _____
_____   _____
_____   _____

PROJECT

_____   _____
_____   _____
_____   _____
_____   _____
_____   _____
_____   _____
_____   _____

PROJECT

_____   _____
_____   _____
_____   _____
_____   _____
_____   _____
_____   _____

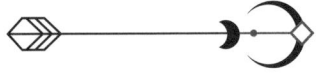

March
Project Breakdown

1. Get into your *ritual for planning* space.

2. Gather the projects from the Quarterly Breakdown that pertain to this month and write each one on a PROJECT line below.

3. Under the project name, enter all of the tasks that are involved in the project. Each of these tasks must be a single action step so that it can be put into your calendar and when you see it, no analysis needs to occur – you know exactly what to do.

_____
PROJECT

_____	_____
_____	_____
_____	_____
_____	_____
_____	_____
_____	_____

_____
PROJECT

_____	_____
_____	_____
_____	_____
_____	_____
_____	_____

48

PROJECT

PROJECT

PROJECT

Weekly Alignment

Top 3 Goals

Finalize Marketing Plan

Research Fundraising

Lose Three Pounds

Focus

Increase Productivity by making sure my health comes first.

Rituals For Thriving

- ✗ EXERCISE
- ✗ MEDITATE / BREATHE
- ✗ JOURNAL
- ○ DANCE
- ✗ GO ON A DATE
- ○ CONNECT WITH NATURE
- ○ VISUALIZE
- ✗ FAMILY TIME
- ✗ COOK / EAT A HEALTHY MEAL
- ○ ORGANIZE MY SPACE / LIFE
- ○ GET RID OF THINGS I DON'T LOVE
- ○ BE WITH FRIENDS
- ✗ PLAY
- ○ LET GO / FORGIVE
- ○ SING / MAKE MUSIC
- ○ CREATE ART
- ✗ READ FOR ENJOYMENT
- ○ CONNECT / PRAY
- ○ CALL SOMEONE / WRITE A LETTER
- ✗ STRETCH / DO YOGA
- ○ MASSAGE / EXCHANGE TOUCH
- ○ SERVE MY COMMUNITY
- ✗ TECHNOLOGY BREAK

Habit Tracking

⬡ = Rode my bike today (measured in miles)

○ = Felt productive (Scale of 1-10)

☐ = Kept my space clean and organized

✧ = Refrained from eating unhealthy snacks

RITUALS FOR LIVING CHALLENGE

{ THIS WEEK, LISTEN TO YOUR INNER GUIDE. YOU HAVE A GREAT KNOWING INSIDE OF YOU THAT CAN: LEAD THE WAY IN TIMES OF CONFLICT, GUIDE YOU TO THE NEXT BEST STEP, AND HELP YOU MAKE HUGE DECISIONS. }

Wins from last week (what I gained / how I grew)

I learned how to be better at saving my energy for what is most important.

I became more aware of the things that do not serve me.

On Sunday, I had an experience that taught me what is most sacred in my life.

How will I reframe something I find difficult, painful, or stressful?

I have been feeling burdened by all the things I'm responsible for, but I've been agreeing to take on more projects even though I don't have the bandwidth. I'm going to use this as an opportunity to get better at saying no and to only make agreements I know I can keep without compromising my peace and health.

How will I create more freedom in my life this week?

This week I forgive myself for my past mistakes, and keep in mind that they were the learning experience that finally brought me to this beautiful place in my life.

Capture Your Brilliance - Dream, Expand, Record, Reflect.

GOOD DEEDS

- ☒ Meditate
- ☒ Surprise my kids
- ☐ Plant a tree
- ☒ Pick up trash I find
- ☒ Say I love you 5x a day
- ☐ Donate those old clothes
- ☒ Call a distant relative
- ☒ Do an unexpected favor at work
- ☒ Make a stranger smile

YOGA POSES THIS WEEK!

- ☒ Warrior I & II
- ☒ Pigeon Pose
- ☒ Plow Pose
- ☒ Camel Pose
- ☒ Bridge Pose
- ☒ Dolphin Pose
- ☒ End w. Savasana

I LOVE MYSELF

Plan that dream vacation already!

DREAM

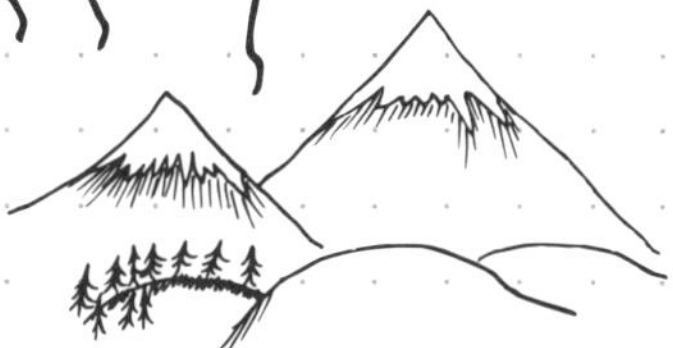

FRIDAYS!

IDEAS!

use your time more wisely!

WEEKEND FUN!

Bring your camera along!

PRAY FOR SUN!

Get out and take advantage of the nice weather

CLEVER LIKE A FOX

50

Bike ride goal: 50 miles this weekend!

Tasks

- MONTHLY PLAN
- INCOMPLETE FROM LAST WEEK
- LIFE DUTIES
- ★ STAR THE MOST IMPORTANT TASKS

INCOMPLETE:
- Lose 3 pounds *
- Clean fridge
- Clean home office *
- Account follow-ups

MONTHLY PLAN:
- Go for 50 miles on weekend bike ride
- Develop biz plan*
- Prep more meals
- Make more time for family & friends *
- Make sure kids get all homework done
- Stretch daily
- Meditate daily
- Look in mirror less
- Start reading that new novel
- Keep workspace clean and tidy *

LIFE DUTIES:
- Laundry on weekend
- Write out budget
- Pay that car bill
- Start taxes
Plan out week meals:
M: Casserole
T: Veggie burgers
W: Eggplant parm
TH: Thai take-out
F: Chicken paprikash
S: Salmon and salad
S: Pizza night!

Final task: schedule next week!
NOW, PUT THESE TASKS & RITUALS IN YOUR CALENDAR
GO FORTH AND BE AWESOME!

| JANUARY 2, 2023 | JANUARY 3, 2023 | JANUARY 4, 2023 |
MONDAY	TUESDAY	WEDNESDAY
INTENTION: Work Hard!	INTENTION: Feel The Love!	INTENTION: Be the best at what you do!
700 wake up happy	700 wake refreshed	700 wake grateful
730 fruit breakfast	730 protein breakfast	730 fruit breakfast
800 bike exercise	800 bike to work	800 bike to work
830 stop for coffee	830 at work early	830 stop for coffee
900 work hard!!!	900 get on the phone and make things happen!	900 start work
- Organize before doing anything else.		
CALL PARTNER FOR MORE FUNDRAISING TIPS!!!	GET AT LEAST FIVE NEW LEADS TODAY	PREPARE INVESTOR REPORTS
WHAT SHALL I BE FOCUSED ON?	WHERE IS MY ATTENTION GOING?	WHAT PERSPECTIVE DO I CHOOSE?
500 bike home	500 bike home	500 bike home
530 get a smoothie	530 home	530 get a smoothie
600 home	MEDITATION TIME!	600 home
- STRETCH *		6:30 knock out bills
700 prepare for date	700 chores	700 cook dinner
730 go out on a date	730 eat dinner	730 eat w. family
800 out to dinner, Have fun, RELAX!	800 play time w. kids - no sitting. get up!	800 study time help w. homework
900 home, kids to bed	900 kids to bed	900 kids to bed
930 read about spirituality	930 read about marketing trends	930 read about travel destinations
1030 get ready for bedtime NO CELLPHONE!	1030 get ready for bedtime FULL EIGHT HOURS!	1030 get ready for bedtime USE JOURNAL!
I AM GRATEFUL FOR:	I AM GRATEFUL FOR:	I AM GRATEFUL FOR:
my beautiful friends!	great weather	my bicycle
my amazing family!	new endeavors	my kids!!!
Health and Prosperity	Strength	my newfound energy
the beauty of nature	Being In Love!	a warm bed at night
songs from my youth	Passion	the Future

2 8 X X   13 9 X X   14 8 X X

JANUARY 5, 2023 THURSDAY	JANUARY 6 2023 FRIDAY	JANUARY 7, 2023 SATURDAY	JANUARY 8, 2023 SUNDAY
INTENTION: Soak up all the healthy vibes!	INTENTION: Burn Fat!	INTENTION: Drink water all day long!	INTENTION: Play like you are a kid again!
700 wake up pumped 730 protein breakfast 800 drive today Drink Tea 900 get it going! – Respond to all the emails twice: now and again at 4pm FOCUS EXTRA HARD TODAY	630 wake up early 730 at the gym 800 switch to cardio 830 shower 900 get to work now – Make sure you have what you need accomplished by end of day for Monday FOLLOW UP ON NEW ACCOUNTS	900 sleep in & relax 930 morning jog 1030 mow the lawn 1100 make brunch 1130 eat w. family 1200 weekend chores 1230 dishes 100 laundry 130 200 vacuum 230 dust 300 clean fridge! 330 drive to the mountains with family & friends for sunset	800 coffee time 8:30 breakfast 900 family time – painting and crafts – puzzle or board games 1200 prep bike 1230 long bike ride 400 back home 430 snack 500 get fam ready
HOW AM I SPENDING MY ENERGY?	HOW DO I AFFECT MY WORLD?	WHAT COULD I LET GO OF?	WHAT IS WORKING WELL FOR ME?
500 drive home 530 pick up dinner 600 eat take–out 6:30 meditate 700 technology break ABSOLUTELY NO TELEVISION!! 830 chores – laundry 900 kids to bed 930 read your new romance novel 1030 get ready for bedtime w. yoga nidra meditation	500 drive home 5/5 get a smoothie 5:30 home – STRETCH * 700 cook dinner 730 eat healthy meal 800 family time – no sitting. get up! 900 kids to bed 930 snuggle up to watch a film. 1200 get ready for bedtime, late night reading for enjoyment?	700 cook dinner 730 eat 800 family time – no sitting. get up! 900 kids to bed 930 wrap up chores: 1000 clean office 1030 fold laundry 1100 write in journal 1130 get ready for bedtime REMEMBER THE GREAT DAY YOU JUST HAD!	530 movie theater 7:30 to pizzeria 800 pizza night! NOT TOO MUCH PIZZA * (maybe salad?) 930 kids to bed 1000 relaxing bath 1100 ready for bed make sure to really RELAX!
I AM GRATEFUL FOR: my awesome job! my Creativity new books to read Fridays... this new comforter	I AM GRATEFUL FOR: my body my face my brain my sharp eyesight my superb hearing	I AM GRATEFUL FOR: weekend fun time with my family giving ME a break! tomorrows bike ride! my wonderful life :)	I AM GRATEFUL FOR: A jam packed week Losing three pounds! exhausting myself reaching new goals embracing next week!

0 7 □ ⬡   0 10 □ X   0 3 X X   24 8 X ⬡

JANUARY

Monday	Tuesday	Wednesday
(26)	(27)	(28)
2	3	4
9	10	11
16 Martin Luther King Jr. Day	17	18
23 30	24 Belly Laugh Day 31	25

Notes:

Thursday	Friday	Saturday	Sunday
(29)	(30)	(31)	1 New Year's Day
5	6 ○	7 Orthodox Christmas	8
12	13	14 ◑	15
19	20 ♒ Aquarius	21 ●	22 Chinese New Year
26 Australia Day Vasant Panchami	27	28 ◐	29

●: New Moon ◑: First Quarter ○: Full Moon ◐: Third Quarter

Dates for moon phases are based on the Eastern Time Zone of the United States. In other parts of the world these phases may technically occur on the previous or following day. If precision is a concern, we encourage you to consult a moon phase calendar specific to your time zone.

Top 3 Goals

Focus

Weekly Alignment

Rituals For Thriving

- EXERCISE
- MEDITATE / BREATHE
- JOURNAL
- DANCE
- GO ON A DATE
- CONNECT WITH NATURE
- VISUALIZE
- FAMILY TIME
- COOK / EAT A HEALTHY MEAL
- ORGANIZE MY SPACE / LIFE
- GET RID OF THINGS I DON'T LOV
- BE WITH FRIENDS
- PLAY
- LET GO / FORGIVE
- SING / MAKE MUSIC
- CREATE ART
- READ FOR ENJOYMENT
- CONNECT / PRAY
- CALL SOMEONE / WRITE A LETT
- STRETCH / DO YOGA
- MASSAGE / EXCHANGE TOUCH
- SERVE MY COMMUNITY
- TECHNOLOGY BREAK

Habit Tracking

◯ = _____
◯ = _____
☐ = _____
⬡ = _____

RITUALS FOR LIVING CHALLENGE

{ SLEEP OPTIMIZATION. GET AT LEAST 7 HOURS EVERY NIGHT. WIND DOWN BEFORE BED WITH DIM LIGHTS AND QUIET. NO SCREENS BEFORE OR IN BED. KEEP YOUR ROOM DARK AND COOL, NO LIGHTS IF YOU GET UP IN THE NIGHT. SLEEP TIGHT. }

Wins from last week (what I gained / how I grew)

_____
_____
_____

How will I reframe something I find difficult, painful, or stressful?

_____
_____
_____

How will I create more freedom in my life this week?

_____
_____

Capture Your Brilliance - Dream, Expand, Record, Reflect:

Routinely let go of anything - physical, mental or emotional - that isn't serving you.

- The Well Life Book

Tasks

- MONTHLY PLAN
- INCOMPLETE FROM LAST WEEK
- LIFE DUTIES
- ★ STAR THE MOST IMPORTANT TASKS

DECEMBER 26, 2022	DECEMBER 27, 2022	DECEMBER 28, 2022
MONDAY	TUESDAY	WEDNESDAY
INTENTION:	INTENTION:	INTENTION:
:	:	:
:	:	:
:	:	:
:	:	:
:	:	:
:	:	:
:	:	:
:	:	:
:	:	:
:	:	:
:	:	:
:	:	:
:	:	:
:	:	:
WHAT SHALL I BE FOCUSED ON?	WHERE IS MY ATTENTION GOING?	WHAT PERSPECTIVE DO I CHOOSE
:	:	:
:	:	:
:	:	:
:	:	:
:	:	:
:	:	:
:	:	:
:	:	:
:	:	:
:	:	:
:	:	:
:	:	:
I AM GRATEFUL FOR:	I AM GRATEFUL FOR:	I AM GRATEFUL FOR:

Final task: schedule next week!
NOW, PUT THESE TASKS & RITUALS
IN YOUR CALENDAR,
GO FORTH AND BE AWESOME!

DECEMBER 29, 2022	DECEMBER 30, 2022	DECEMBER 31, 2022	JANUARY 1, 2023
THURSDAY	FRIDAY	SATURDAY	SUNDAY
INTENTION:	INTENTION:	INTENTION:	INTENTION:
:	:	:	:
:	:	:	:
:	:	:	:
:	:	:	:
:	:	:	:
:	:	:	:
:	:	:	:
:	:	:	:
:	:	:	:
:	:	:	:
:	:	:	:
:	:	:	:
:	:	:	:
:	:	:	:
:	:	:	:
:	:	:	:
HOW AM I SPENDING MY ENERGY?	HOW DO I AFFECT MY WORLD?	WHAT COULD I LET GO OF?	WHAT IS WORKING WELL FOR ME?
:	:	:	:
:	:	:	:
:	:	:	:
:	:	:	:
:	:	:	:
:	:	:	:
:	:	:	:
:	:	:	:
:	:	:	:
:	:	:	:
:	:	:	:
:	:	:	:
:	:	:	:
I AM GRATEFUL FOR:	I AM GRATEFUL FOR:	I AM GRATEFUL FOR:	I AM GRATEFUL FOR:

Top 3 Goals

_____

_____

_____

Weekly Alignment

Focus

Habit Tracking

◯ = _____

◯ = _____

▢ = _____

✦ = _____

Rituals For Thriving

- ○ EXERCISE
- ○ MEDITATE / BREATHE
- ○ JOURNAL
- ○ DANCE
- ○ GO ON A DATE
- ○ CONNECT WITH NATURE
- ○ VISUALIZE
- ○ FAMILY TIME
- ○ COOK / EAT A HEALTHY MEAL
- ○ ORGANIZE MY SPACE / LIFE
- ○ GET RID OF THINGS I DON'T LOV
- ○ BE WITH FRIENDS
- ○ PLAY
- ○ LET GO / FORGIVE
- ○ SING / MAKE MUSIC
- ○ CREATE ART
- ○ READ FOR ENJOYMENT
- ○ CONNECT / PRAY
- ○ CALL SOMEONE / WRITE A LET
- ○ STRETCH / DO YOGA
- ○ MASSAGE / EXCHANGE TOUCH
- ○ SERVE MY COMMUNITY
- ○ TECHNOLOGY BREAK

RITUALS FOR LIVING CHALLENGE

{ THIS WEEK, BUY AS LITTLE IN PLASTIC CONTAINERS AS POSSIBLE. PLASTICS CAN DISRUPT YOUR ENDOCRINE SYSTEM, AND ARE EXTREMELY PERSISTENT IN THE ENVIRONMENT. MOST TAP WATER IS SAFE OR CAN BE EASILY MADE CLEAN WITH A FILTER. }

Wins from last week (what I gained / how I grew)

_____

_____

_____

How will I reframe something I find difficult, painful, or stressful?

_____

_____

_____

How will I create more freedom in my life this week?

_____

_____

Capture Your Brilliance - Dream, Expand, Record, Reflect:

Tasks

- MONTHLY PLAN
- INCOMPLETE FROM LAST WEEK
- LIFE DUTIES
- ★ STAR THE MOST IMPORTANT TASKS

JANUARY 2, 2023	JANUARY 3, 2023	JANUARY 4, 2023
MONDAY	**TUESDAY**	**WEDNESDAY**
INTENTION:	INTENTION:	INTENTION:
:	:	:
:	:	:
:	:	:
:	:	:
:	:	:
:	:	:
:	:	:
:	:	:
:	:	:
:	:	:
:	:	:
:	:	:
:	:	:
:	:	:
:	:	:
WHAT SHALL I BE FOCUSED ON?	WHERE IS MY ATTENTION GOING?	WHAT PERSPECTIVE DO I CHOOSE
:	:	:
:	:	:
:	:	:
:	:	:
:	:	:
:	:	:
:	:	:
:	:	:
:	:	:
:	:	:
:	:	:
:	:	:
:	:	:
I AM GRATEFUL FOR:	I AM GRATEFUL FOR:	I AM GRATEFUL FOR:

Final task: schedule next week!
NOW, PUT THESE TASKS & RITUALS
IN YOUR CALENDAR,
GO FORTH AND BE AWESOME!

62

JANUARY 5, 2023	JANUARY 6, 2023	JANUARY 7, 2023	JANUARY 8, 2023
THURSDAY	FRIDAY ⚪	SATURDAY	SUNDAY
INTENTION:	INTENTION:	INTENTION:	INTENTION:
:	:	:	:
:	:	:	:
:	:	:	:
:	:	:	:
:	:	:	:
:	:	:	:
:	:	:	:
:	:	:	:
:	:	:	:
:	:	:	:
:	:	:	:
:	:	:	:
:	:	:	:
:	:	:	:
:	:	:	
HOW AM I SPENDING MY ENERGY?	HOW DO I AFFECT MY WORLD?	WHAT COULD I LET GO OF?	WHAT IS WORKING WELL FOR ME?
:	:	:	:
:	:	:	:
.	:	.	.
:	:	:	:
:	:	:	:
:	:	:	:
:	:	:	:
:	:	:	:
:	:	:	:
:	:	:	:
:	:	:	:
:	:	:	:
:	:	:	:
I AM GRATEFUL FOR:	I AM GRATEFUL FOR:	I AM GRATEFUL FOR:	I AM GRATEFUL FOR:

Top 3 Goals

Weekly Alignment

Focus

Rituals For Thriving

- EXERCISE
- MEDITATE / BREATHE
- JOURNAL
- DANCE
- GO ON A DATE
- CONNECT WITH NATURE
- VISUALIZE
- FAMILY TIME
- COOK / EAT A HEALTHY MEAL
- ORGANIZE MY SPACE / LIFE
- GET RID OF THINGS I DON'T LO
- BE WITH FRIENDS
- PLAY
- LET GO / FORGIVE
- SING / MAKE MUSIC
- CREATE ART
- READ FOR ENJOYMENT
- CONNECT / PRAY
- CALL SOMEONE / WRITE A LET
- STRETCH / DO YOGA
- MASSAGE / EXCHANGE TOUCH
- SERVE MY COMMUNITY
- TECHNOLOGY BREAK

Habit Tracking

⬡ = _____

◯ = _____

▢ = _____

✧ = _____

RITUALS FOR LIVING CHALLENGE

{ THIS WEEK, CREATE OR REFINE YOUR "SACRED SPACE." A PLACE FOR YOU TO TUNE IN, CENTER YOURSELF, GET GROUNDED, MEDITATE, AND VISUALIZE. MAKE IT APPEALING AND CONDUCIVE TO PEACE. }

Wins from last week (what I gained / how I grew)

How will I reframe something I find difficult, painful, or stressful?

How will I create more freedom in my life this week?

Capture Your Brilliance - Dream, Expand, Record, Reflect.

Don't let others' opinions define your value or dictate your self-esteem.

- The Well Life Book

Tasks

- MONTHLY PLAN
- INCOMPLETE FROM LAST WEEK
- LIFE DUTIES
- ★ STAR THE MOST IMPORTANT TASKS

JANUARY 9, 2023	JANUARY 10, 2023	JANUARY 11, 2023
MONDAY	TUESDAY	WEDNESDAY
INTENTION:	INTENTION:	INTENTION:
:	:	:
:	:	:
:	:	:
:	:	:
:	:	:
:	:	:
:	:	:
:	:	:
:	:	:
:	:	:
:	:	:
:	:	:
:	:	:
:	:	:
WHAT SHALL I BE FOCUSED ON?	WHERE IS MY ATTENTION GOING?	WHAT PERSPECTIVE DO I CHOOSE?
:	:	:
:	:	:
:	:	:
:	:	:
:	:	:
:	:	:
:	:	:
:	:	:
:	:	:
:	:	:
:	:	:
:	:	:
:	:	:
I AM GRATEFUL FOR:	I AM GRATEFUL FOR:	I AM GRATEFUL FOR:

Final task: schedule next week!
NOW, PUT THESE TASKS & RITUALS
IN YOUR CALENDAR.
GO FORTH AND BE AWESOME!

JANUARY 12, 2023	JANUARY 13, 2023	JANUARY 14, 2023	JANUARY 15, 2023
THURSDAY	FRIDAY	SATURDAY ◑	SUNDAY
INTENTION:	INTENTION:	INTENTION:	INTENTION:

:	:	:	:
:	:	:	:
:	:	:	:
:	:	:	:
:	:	:	:
:	:	:	:
:	:	:	:
:	:	:	:
:	:	:	:
:	:	:	:
:	:	:	:
:	:	:	:
:	:	:	:
:	:	:	:
:	:	:	:
:	:	:	:

HOW AM I SPENDING MY ENERGY?	HOW DO I AFFECT MY WORLD?	WHAT COULD I LET GO OF?	WHAT IS WORKING WELL FOR ME?
:	:	:	:
:	:	:	:
:	:	:	:
:	:	:	:
:	:	:	:
:	:	:	:
:	:	:	:
:	:	:	:
:	:	:	:
:	:	:	:
:	:	:	:
:	:	:	:

I AM GRATEFUL FOR:	I AM GRATEFUL FOR:	I AM GRATEFUL FOR:	I AM GRATEFUL FOR:

Top 3 Goals

_____

_____

_____

Weekly Alignment

Focus

Habit Tracking

⬡ = _____

◯ = _____

▢ = _____

✷ = _____

RITUALS FOR LIVING CHALLENGE

{ THIS WEEK, PAY SPECIAL ATTENTION TO YOUR POSTURE. TUCK YOUR CHIN A BIT AND LIFT THE TOP OF YOUR HEAD AS IF YOU WERE BEING SUSPENDED BY A STRING. LET YOUR CHEST AND HEART OPEN. CARRY YOURSELF WITH PURPOSE. CHANGE YOUR WORK STATION IF NECESSARY. }

Rituals For Thrivin

- o EXERCISE
- o MEDITATE / BREATHE
- o JOURNAL
- o DANCE
- o GO ON A DATE
- o CONNECT WITH NATURE
- o VISUALIZE
- o FAMILY TIME
- o COOK / EAT A HEALTHY MEAL
- o ORGANIZE MY SPACE / LIFE
- o GET RID OF THINGS I DON'T LO
- o BE WITH FRIENDS
- o PLAY
- o LET GO / FORGIVE
- o SING / MAKE MUSIC
- o CREATE ART
- o READ FOR ENJOYMENT
- o CONNECT / PRAY
- o CALL SOMEONE / WRITE A LET
- o STRETCH / DO YOGA
- o MASSAGE / EXCHANGE TOUCH
- o SERVE MY COMMUNITY
- o TECHNOLOGY BREAK

Wins from last week (what I gained / how I grew)

_____

_____

How will I reframe something I find difficult, painful, or stressful?

_____

_____

How will I create more freedom in my life this week?

_____

_____

Capture Your Brilliance - Dream, Expand, Record, Reflect:

Tasks

- MONTHLY PLAN
- INCOMPLETE FROM LAST WEEK
- LIFE DUTIES
- ★ STAR THE MOST IMPORTANT TASKS

JANUARY 16, 2023	JANUARY 17, 2023	JANUARY 18, 2023
MONDAY	TUESDAY	WEDNESDAY
INTENTION:	INTENTION:	INTENTION:
:	:	:
:	:	:
:	:	:
:	:	:
:	:	:
:	:	:
:	:	:
:	:	:
:	:	:
:	:	:
:	:	:
:	:	:
:	:	:
:	:	:
WHAT SHALL I BE FOCUSED ON?	WHERE IS MY ATTENTION GOING?	WHAT PERSPECTIVE DO I CHOOSE?
:	:	:
:	:	:
:	:	:
:	:	:
:	:	:
:	:	:
:	:	:
:	:	:
:	:	:
:	:	:
:	:	:
I AM GRATEFUL FOR:	I AM GRATEFUL FOR:	I AM GRATEFUL FOR:

Final task: schedule next week!
NOW, PUT THESE TASKS & RITUALS
IN YOUR CALENDAR.
GO FORTH AND BE AWESOME!

JANUARY 19, 2023	JANUARY 20, 2023	JANUARY 21, 2023	JANUARY 22, 2023
THURSDAY	FRIDAY	SATURDAY ●	SUNDAY
INTENTION:	INTENTION:	INTENTION:	INTENTION:
:	:	:	:
:	:	:	:
:	:	:	:
:	:	:	:
:	:	:	:
:	:	:	:
:	:	:	:
:	:	:	:
:	:	:	:
:	:	:	:
:	:	:	:
:	:	:	:
:	:	:	:
:	:	:	:
:	:	:	:
:	:	:	:
HOW AM I SPENDING MY ENERGY?	HOW DO I AFFECT MY WORLD?	WHAT COULD I LET GO OF?	WHAT IS WORKING WELL FOR ME?
:	:	:	:
:	:	:	:
:	:	:	:
:	:	:	:
:	:	:	:
:	:	:	:
:	:	:	:
:	:	:	:
:	:	:	:
:	:	:	:
:	:	:	:
I AM GRATEFUL FOR:	I AM GRATEFUL FOR:	I AM GRATEFUL FOR:	I AM GRATEFUL FOR:

Top 3 Goals

_____

_____

_____

Weekly Alignment

Focus

Habit Tracking

◯ = _____

◯ = _____

☐ = _____

✦ = _____

Rituals For Thriving

- ○ EXERCISE
- ○ MEDITATE / BREATHE
- ○ JOURNAL
- ○ DANCE
- ○ GO ON A DATE
- ○ CONNECT WITH NATURE
- ○ VISUALIZE
- ○ FAMILY TIME
- ○ COOK / EAT A HEALTHY MEAL
- ○ ORGANIZE MY SPACE / LIFE
- ○ GET RID OF THINGS I DON'T LOVE
- ○ BE WITH FRIENDS
- ○ PLAY
- ○ LET GO / FORGIVE
- ○ SING / MAKE MUSIC
- ○ CREATE ART
- ○ READ FOR ENJOYMENT
- ○ CONNECT / PRAY
- ○ CALL SOMEONE / WRITE A LETTER
- ○ STRETCH / DO YOGA
- ○ MASSAGE / EXCHANGE TOUCH
- ○ SERVE MY COMMUNITY
- ○ TECHNOLOGY BREAK

RITUALS FOR LIVING CHALLENGE

{ THIS WEEK, HYDRATE. DIVIDE THE NUMBER OF POUNDS YOU WEIGH IN HALF AND DRINK THAT MANY OUNCES OF WATER EACH DAY. METRIC: YOUR WEIGHT IN KG, DIVIDE BY 30, DRINK THAT MANY LITERS OF WATER PER DAY. }

Wins from last week (what I gained / how I grew)

_____

_____

_____

How will I reframe something I find difficult, painful, or stressful?

_____

_____

_____

How will I create more freedom in my life this week?

_____

_____

Capture Your Brilliance - Dream, Expand, Record, Reflect:

Hold space for life to just be - without the need to resist it, cling to it, or change it.
- The Well Life Book

Tasks

- MONTHLY PLAN
- INCOMPLETE FROM LAST WEEK
- LIFE DUTIES
- ★ STAR THE MOST IMPORTANT TASKS

JANUARY 23, 2023	JANUARY 24, 2023	JANUARY 25, 2023
MONDAY	TUESDAY	WEDNESDAY
INTENTION:	INTENTION:	INTENTION:
:	:	:
:	:	:
:	:	:
:	:	:
:	:	:
:	:	:
:	:	:
:	:	:
:	:	:
:	:	:
:	:	:
:	:	:
:	:	:
:	:	:
WHAT SHALL I BE FOCUSED ON?	WHERE IS MY ATTENTION GOING?	WHAT PERSPECTIVE DO I CHOOSE?
:	:	:
:	:	:
:	:	:
:	:	:
:	:	:
:	:	:
:	:	:
:	:	:
:	:	:
:	:	:
:	:	:
:	:	:
:	:	:
I AM GRATEFUL FOR:	I AM GRATEFUL FOR:	I AM GRATEFUL FOR:

Final task: schedule next week!
NOW, PUT THESE TASKS & RITUALS
IN YOUR CALENDAR.
GO FORTH AND BE AWESOME!

JANUARY 26, 2023	JANUARY 27, 2023	JANUARY 28, 2023	JANUARY 29, 2023
THURSDAY	FRIDAY	SATURDAY ◑	SUNDAY
INTENTION:	INTENTION:	INTENTION:	INTENTION:
:	:	:	:
:	:	:	:
:	:	:	:
:	:	:	:
:	:	:	:
:	:	:	:
:	:	:	:
:	:	:	:
:	:	:	:
:	:	:	:
:	:	:	:
:	:	:	:
:	:	:	:
:	:	:	:
:	:	:	:
HOW AM I SPENDING MY ENERGY?	HOW DO I AFFECT MY WORLD?	WHAT COULD I LET GO OF?	WHAT IS WORKING WELL FOR ME?
:	:	:	:
:	:	:	:
:	:	:	:
:	:	:	:
:	:	:	:
:	:	:	:
:	:	:	:
:	:	:	:
:	:	:	:
:	:	:	:
:	:	:	:
:	:	:	:
:	:	:	:
I AM GRATEFUL FOR:	I AM GRATEFUL FOR:	I AM GRATEFUL FOR:	I AM GRATEFUL FOR:

FEBRUARY

Monday	Tuesday	Wednesday
(30)	(31)	1
6 Waitangi Day (NZ)	7	8
13 ◑	14 Valentine's Day	15
20 President's Day ●	21	22
27 ◐	28	(1)

Notes:

Thursday	Friday	Saturday	Sunday
2	3	4	5 ○
9	10	11	12
16	17	18 Maha Shivaratri ♓ Pisces	19
23	24	25	26
(2)	(3)	(4)	(5)

●: New Moon ◐: First Quarter ○: Full Moon ◑: Third Quarter

Dates for moon phases are based on the Eastern Time Zone of the United States. In other parts of the world these phases may technically occur on the previous or following day. If precision is a concern, we encourage you to consult a moon phase calendar specific to your time zone.

Top 3 Goals

_____

_____

_____

Weekly Alignment

Focus

Habit Tracking

⬡ = _____

◯ = _____

▢ = _____

✦ = _____

RITUALS FOR LIVING CHALLENGE

{ THIS WEEK, TAKE A DRAMA FAST. ABSTAIN FROM GOSSIP, COMPLAINING, CATASTROPHIZING, SENSATIONALIZING. TELL YOUR FRIENDS YOU SYMPATHIZE BUT AREN'T GOING THERE. AVOID THE NEWS, OR AT LEAST THE TRAGIC STUFF. }

Rituals For Thriving

- ○ EXERCISE
- ○ MEDITATE / BREATHE
- ○ JOURNAL
- ○ DANCE
- ○ GO ON A DATE
- ○ CONNECT WITH NATURE
- ○ VISUALIZE
- ○ FAMILY TIME
- ○ COOK / EAT A HEALTHY MEAL
- ○ ORGANIZE MY SPACE / LIFE
- ○ GET RID OF THINGS I DON'T LOV
- ○ BE WITH FRIENDS
- ○ PLAY
- ○ LET GO / FORGIVE
- ○ SING / MAKE MUSIC
- ○ CREATE ART
- ○ READ FOR ENJOYMENT
- ○ CONNECT / PRAY
- ○ CALL SOMEONE / WRITE A LETT
- ○ STRETCH / DO YOGA
- ○ MASSAGE / EXCHANGE TOUCH
- ○ SERVE MY COMMUNITY
- ○ TECHNOLOGY BREAK

Wins from last week (what I gained / how I grew)

_____

_____

_____

How will I reframe something I find difficult, painful, or stressful?

_____

_____

_____

How will I create more freedom in my life this week?

_____

_____

Capture Your Brilliance - Dream, Expand, Record, Reflect:

Tasks

- MONTHLY PLAN
- INCOMPLETE FROM LAST WEEK
- LIFE DUTIES
- ★ STAR THE MOST IMPORTANT TASKS

JANUARY 30, 2023	JANUARY 31, 2023	FEBRUARY 1, 2023
MONDAY	TUESDAY	WEDNESDAY
INTENTION:	INTENTION:	INTENTION:
:	:	:
:	:	:
:	:	:
:	:	:
:	:	:
:	:	:
:	:	:
:	:	:
:	:	:
:	:	:
:	:	:
:	:	:
:	:	:
:	:	:
WHAT SHALL I BE FOCUSED ON?	WHERE IS MY ATTENTION GOING?	WHAT PERSPECTIVE DO I CHOOSE?
:	:	:
:	:	:
:	:	:
:	:	:
:	:	:
:	:	:
:	:	:
:	:	:
:	:	:
:	:	:
:	:	:
:	:	:
:	:	:
I AM GRATEFUL FOR:	I AM GRATEFUL FOR:	I AM GRATEFUL FOR:

Final task: schedule next week!
NOW, PUT THESE TASKS & RITUALS
IN YOUR CALENDAR,
GO FORTH AND BE AWESOME!

FEBRUARY 2, 2023	FEBRUARY 3, 2023	FEBRUARY 4, 2023	FEBRUARY 5, 2023
THURSDAY	FRIDAY	SATURDAY	SUNDAY ○
INTENTION:	INTENTION:	INTENTION:	INTENTION:
:	:	:	:
:	:	:	:
:	:	:	:
:	:	:	:
:	:	:	:
:	:	:	:
:	:	:	:
:	:	:	:
:	:	:	:
:	:	:	:
:	:	:	:
:	:	:	:
:	:	:	:
:	:	:	:
:	:	:	:
HOW AM I SPENDING MY ENERGY?	HOW DO I AFFECT MY WORLD?	WHAT COULD I LET GO OF?	WHAT IS WORKING WELL FOR ME?
:	:	:	:
:	:	:	:
:	:	:	:
:	:	:	:
:	:	:	:
:	:	:	:
:	:	:	:
:	:	:	:
:	:	:	:
:	:	:	:
:	:	:	:
:	:	:	:
I AM GRATEFUL FOR:	I AM GRATEFUL FOR:	I AM GRATEFUL FOR:	I AM GRATEFUL FOR:

Top 3 Goals

_____

_____

Weekly Alignment

Focus

Habit Tracking

⬡ = _____

◯ = _____

▢ = _____

✦ = _____

Rituals For Thriving

o   EXERCISE
o   MEDITATE / BREATHE
o   JOURNAL
o   DANCE
o   GO ON A DATE
o   CONNECT WITH NATURE
o   VISUALIZE
o   FAMILY TIME
o   COOK / EAT A HEALTHY MEAL
o   ORGANIZE MY SPACE / LIFE
o   GET RID OF THINGS I DON'T LOV
o   BE WITH FRIENDS
o   PLAY
o   LET GO / FORGIVE
o   SING / MAKE MUSIC
o   CREATE ART
o   READ FOR ENJOYMENT
o   CONNECT / PRAY
o   CALL SOMEONE / WRITE A LETT
o   STRETCH / DO YOGA
o   MASSAGE / EXCHANGE TOUCH
o   SERVE MY COMMUNITY
o   TECHNOLOGY BREAK

RITUALS FOR LIVING CHALLENGE

{ THIS WEEK, TREAT EVERYONE YOU MEET –
BANK TELLERS, FRIENDS, CASHIERS – AS IF THEY
ARE AN ENLIGHTENED BEING. AS IF THEY HAVE
SOMETHING PROFOUND TO SHARE WITH YOU.
AS IF THEY HAVE SHOWN UP IN YOUR LIFE TO
TEACH OR REMIND YOU OF SOMETHING. }

Wins from last week (what I gained / how I grew)

_____

_____

_____

How will I reframe something I find difficult, painful, or stressful?

_____

_____

_____

How will I create more freedom in my life this week?

_____

_____

Capture Your Brilliance - Dream, Expand, Record, Reflect:

Think of your desires like stars - dense ideas that bend reality toward themselves.

- The Well Life Book

Tasks

- MONTHLY PLAN
- INCOMPLETE FROM LAST WEEK
- LIFE DUTIES
- ★ STAR THE MOST IMPORTANT TASKS

FEBRUARY 6, 2023	FEBRUARY 7, 2023	FEBRUARY 8, 2023
MONDAY	TUESDAY	WEDNESDAY
INTENTION:	INTENTION:	INTENTION:
:	:	:
:	:	:
:	:	:
:	:	:
:	:	:
:	:	:
:	:	:
:	:	:
:	:	:
:	:	:
:	:	:
:	:	:
:	:	:
:	:	:
WHAT SHALL I BE FOCUSED ON?	WHERE IS MY ATTENTION GOING?	WHAT PERSPECTIVE DO I CHOOSE?
:	:	:
:	:	:
:	:	:
:	:	:
:	:	:
:	:	:
:	:	:
:	:	:
:	:	:
:	:	:
:	:	:
I AM GRATEFUL FOR:	I AM GRATEFUL FOR:	I AM GRATEFUL FOR:

Final task: schedule next week!
NOW, PUT THESE TASKS & RITUALS
IN YOUR CALENDAR.
GO FORTH AND BE AWESOME!

  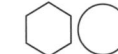 

FEBRUARY 9, 2023	FEBRUARY 10, 2023	FEBRUARY 11, 2023	FEBRUARY 12, 2023
THURSDAY	FRIDAY	SATURDAY	SUNDAY
INTENTION:	INTENTION:	INTENTION:	INTENTION:
:	:	:	:
:	:	:	:
:	:	:	:
:	:	:	:
:	:	:	:
:	:	:	:
:	:	:	:
:	:	:	:
:	:	:	:
:	:	:	:
:	:	:	:
:	:	:	:
:	:	:	:
:	:	:	:
:	:	:	:
:	:	:	:
HOW AM I SPENDING MY ENERGY?	HOW DO I AFFECT MY WORLD?	WHAT COULD I LET GO OF?	WHAT IS WORKING WELL FOR ME?
:	:	:	:
:	:	:	:
:	:	:	:
:	:	:	:
:	:	:	:
:	:	:	:
:	:	:	:
:	:	:	:
:	:	:	:
:	:	:	:
:	:	:	:
:	:	:	:
:	:	:	:
:	:	:	:
I AM GRATEFUL FOR:	I AM GRATEFUL FOR:	I AM GRATEFUL FOR:	I AM GRATEFUL FOR:

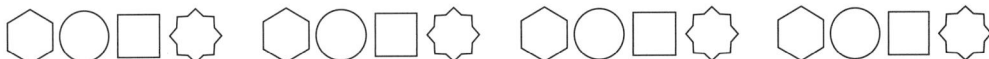

Top 3 Goals

_____

_____

_____

Weekly Alignment

Focus

Rituals For Thriving

- EXERCISE
- MEDITATE / BREATHE
- JOURNAL
- DANCE
- GO ON A DATE
- CONNECT WITH NATURE
- VISUALIZE
- FAMILY TIME
- COOK / EAT A HEALTHY MEAL
- ORGANIZE MY SPACE / LIFE
- GET RID OF THINGS I DON'T LOV
- BE WITH FRIENDS
- PLAY
- LET GO / FORGIVE
- SING / MAKE MUSIC
- CREATE ART
- READ FOR ENJOYMENT
- CONNECT / PRAY
- CALL SOMEONE / WRITE A LETT
- STRETCH / DO YOGA
- MASSAGE / EXCHANGE TOUCH
- SERVE MY COMMUNITY
- TECHNOLOGY BREAK

Habit Tracking

⬡ = _____

◯ = _____

▢ = _____

✦ = _____

RITUALS FOR LIVING CHALLENGE

{ GREEN SMOOTHIE 5 TIMES THIS WEEK: BIG HANDFUL OF SPINACH, HANDFUL OF WHOLE FRUIT (BANANA, MANGO, BERRIES, ETC.), DASH OF LEMON, SLICE OF GINGER, ADD WATER TO MAKE 1 QUART/LITER. (DROP OF HONEY OK.) BLEND UNTIL SMOOTH. DRINK SLOWLY. }

Wins from last week (what I gained / how I grew)

_____

_____

_____

How will I reframe something I find difficult, painful, or stressful?

_____

_____

_____

How will I create more freedom in my life this week?

_____

_____

Capture Your Brilliance - Dream, Expand, Record, Reflect:

Tasks

- MONTHLY PLAN
- INCOMPLETE FROM LAST WEEK
- LIFE DUTIES
- ★ STAR THE MOST IMPORTANT TASKS

FEBRUARY 13, 2023	FEBRUARY 14, 2023	FEBRUARY 15, 2023
MONDAY ◑	TUESDAY	WEDNESDAY
INTENTION:	INTENTION:	INTENTION:
:	:	:
:	:	:
:	:	:
:	:	:
:	:	:
:	:	:
:	:	:
:	:	:
:	:	:
:	:	:
:	:	:
:	:	:
:	:	:
WHAT SHALL I BE FOCUSED ON?	WHERE IS MY ATTENTION GOING?	WHAT PERSPECTIVE DO I CHOOSE?
:	:	:
:	:	:
:	:	:
:	:	:
:	:	:
:	:	:
:	:	:
:	:	:
:	:	:
:	:	:
:	:	:
:	:	:
I AM GRATEFUL FOR:	I AM GRATEFUL FOR:	I AM GRATEFUL FOR:

Final task: schedule next week!
NOW, PUT THESE TASKS & RITUALS
IN YOUR CALENDAR.
GO FORTH AND BE AWESOME!

88

FEBRUARY 16, 2023	FEBRUARY 17, 2023	FEBRUARY 18, 2023	FEBRUARY 19, 2023
THURSDAY	FRIDAY	SATURDAY	SUNDAY
INTENTION:	INTENTION:	INTENTION:	INTENTION:

HOW AM I SPENDING MY ENERGY?	HOW DO I AFFECT MY WORLD?	WHAT COULD I LET GO OF?	WHAT IS WORKING WELL FOR ME?
I AM GRATEFUL FOR:	I AM GRATEFUL FOR:	I AM GRATEFUL FOR:	I AM GRATEFUL FOR:

Top 3 Goals

_____

_____

_____

Weekly Alignment

Focus

Habit Tracking

⬡ = _____

◯ = _____

▢ = _____

✦ = _____

RITUALS FOR LIVING CHALLENGE

{ THIS WEEK, REACH OUT: CONNECT WITH THREE PEOPLE YOU'VE BEEN OUT OF TOUCH WITH. TELL THEM YOU'RE GLAD TO HAVE THEM IN YOUR LIFE. }

Rituals For Thriving

- EXERCISE
- MEDITATE / BREATHE
- JOURNAL
- DANCE
- GO ON A DATE
- CONNECT WITH NATURE
- VISUALIZE
- FAMILY TIME
- COOK / EAT A HEALTHY MEAL
- ORGANIZE MY SPACE / LIFE
- GET RID OF THINGS I DON'T LOV
- BE WITH FRIENDS
- PLAY
- LET GO / FORGIVE
- SING / MAKE MUSIC
- CREATE ART
- READ FOR ENJOYMENT
- CONNECT / PRAY
- CALL SOMEONE / WRITE A LETT
- STRETCH / DO YOGA
- MASSAGE / EXCHANGE TOUCH
- SERVE MY COMMUNITY
- TECHNOLOGY BREAK

Wins from last week (what I gained / how I grew)

_____

_____

_____

How will I reframe something I find difficult, painful, or stressful?

_____

_____

_____

How will I create more freedom in my life this week?

_____

_____

Capture Your Brilliance - Dream, Expand, Record, Reflect:

Whatever you feel, invite the feeling to be felt.

- The Well Life Book

Tasks

- MONTHLY PLAN
- INCOMPLETE FROM LAST WEEK
- LIFE DUTIES
- ★ STAR THE MOST IMPORTANT TASKS

_____
_____
_____
_____
_____
_____
_____
_____
_____
_____
_____
_____
_____
_____
_____
_____
_____
_____
_____
_____
_____
_____
_____
_____
_____
_____
_____
_____
_____
_____
_____
_____
_____
_____
_____
_____
_____
_____

Final task: schedule next week!
NOW, PUT THESE TASKS & RITUALS
IN YOUR CALENDAR,
GO FORTH AND BE AWESOME!

| FEBRUARY 20, 2023 | FEBRUARY 21, 2023 | FEBRUARY 22, 2023 |
MONDAY ●	TUESDAY	WEDNESDAY
INTENTION:	INTENTION:	INTENTION:
:	:	:
:	:	:
:	:	:
:	:	:
:	:	:
:	:	:
:	:	:
:	:	:
:	:	:
:	:	:
:	:	:
:	:	:
:	:	:
:	:	:
:	:	:
:	:	
WHAT SHALL I BE FOCUSED ON?	WHERE IS MY ATTENTION GOING?	WHAT PERSPECTIVE DO I CHOOSE
:	:	:
:	:	:
:	:	:
:	:	:
:	:	:
:	:	:
:	:	:
:	:	:
:	:	:
:	:	:
:	:	:
:	:	:
I AM GRATEFUL FOR:	I AM GRATEFUL FOR:	I AM GRATEFUL FOR:

FEBRUARY 23, 2023	FEBRUARY 24, 2023	FEBRUARY 25, 2023	FEBRUARY 26, 2023
THURSDAY	FRIDAY	SATURDAY	SUNDAY
INTENTION:	INTENTION:	INTENTION:	INTENTION:
:	:	:	:
:	:	:	:
:	:	:	:
:	:	:	:
:	:	:	:
:	:	:	:
:	:	:	:
:	:	:	:
:	:	:	:
:	:	:	:
:	:	:	:
:	:	:	:
:	:	:	:
:	:	:	:
:	:	:	:
:	:	:	:
HOW AM I SPENDING MY ENERGY?	HOW DO I AFFECT MY WORLD?	WHAT COULD I LET GO OF?	WHAT IS WORKING WELL FOR ME?
:	:	:	:
:	:	:	:
:	:	:	:
:	:	:	:
:	:	:	:
:	:	:	:
:	:	:	:
:	:	:	:
:	:	:	:
:	:	:	:
:	:	:	:
:	:	:	:
:	:	:	:
I AM GRATEFUL FOR:	I AM GRATEFUL FOR:	I AM GRATEFUL FOR:	I AM GRATEFUL FOR:

MARCH

Monday	Tuesday	Wednesday
(27)	(28)	1
6	7 Purim ○	8 International Women's Day
13	14 ◐	15
20 Spring Equinox ♈ Aries	21 World Poetry Day ●	22 Start of Ramadan
27	28 ◑	29

Notes:

Thursday	Friday	Saturday	Sunday
2	3	4	5
9	10	11	12 Daylight Savings Begins
16	17 St. Patrick's Day	18	19
23	24	25	26
30	31	(1)	(2)

●: New Moon : First Quarter ○: Full Moon ◑: Third Quarter

ates for moon phases are based on the Eastern Time Zone of the United States. In other parts of the world these phases may technically
cur on the previous or following day. If precision is a concern, we encourage you to consult a moon phase calendar specific to your time zone.

Top 3 Goals

_____

_____

_____

Weekly Alignment

Focus

Habit Tracking

⬡ = _____

◯ = _____

▢ = _____

✺ = _____

Rituals For Thrivin

- ○ EXERCISE
- ○ MEDITATE / BREATHE
- ○ JOURNAL
- ○ DANCE
- ○ GO ON A DATE
- ○ CONNECT WITH NATURE
- ○ VISUALIZE
- ○ FAMILY TIME
- ○ COOK / EAT A HEALTHY MEAL
- ○ ORGANIZE MY SPACE / LIFE
- ○ GET RID OF THINGS I DON'T LO
- ○ BE WITH FRIENDS
- ○ PLAY
- ○ LET GO / FORGIVE
- ○ SING / MAKE MUSIC
- ○ CREATE ART
- ○ READ FOR ENJOYMENT
- ○ CONNECT / PRAY
- ○ CALL SOMEONE / WRITE A LET
- ○ STRETCH / DO YOGA
- ○ MASSAGE / EXCHANGE TOUCH
- ○ SERVE MY COMMUNITY
- ○ TECHNOLOGY BREAK

RITUALS FOR LIVING CHALLENGE

{ THIS WEEK, SERVE. FIND A WAY TO DO SOMETHING IN SERVICE TO YOUR COMMUNITY. EXAMPLES: VOLUNTEER AT A SHELTER, SHOVEL AN ELDERLY NEIGHBOR'S DRIVEWAY, REPAIR A PUBLIC BENCH, PICK UP LITTER ON YOUR MORNING WALK. GET CREATIVE. }

Wins from last week (what I gained / how I grew)

_____

_____

How will I reframe something I find difficult, painful, or stressful?

_____

_____

How will I create more freedom in my life this week?

_____

_____

Capture Your Brilliance - Dream, Expand, Record, Reflect:

Tasks

- MONTHLY PLAN
- INCOMPLETE FROM LAST WEEK
- LIFE DUTIES
- ★ STAR THE MOST IMPORTANT TASKS

FEBRUARY 27, 2023	FEBRUARY 28, 2023	MARCH 1, 2023
MONDAY ◑	TUESDAY	WEDNESDAY
INTENTION:	INTENTION:	INTENTION:
:	:	:
:	:	:
:	:	:
:	:	:
:	:	:
:	:	:
:	:	:
:	:	:
:	:	:
:	:	:
:	:	:
:	:	:
:	:	:
:	:	:
:	:	:
WHAT SHALL I BE FOCUSED ON?	WHERE IS MY ATTENTION GOING?	WHAT PERSPECTIVE DO I CHOOSE?
:	:	:
:	:	:
:	:	:
:	:	:
:	:	:
:	:	:
:	:	:
:	:	:
:	:	:
:	:	:
:	:	:
:	:	:
I AM GRATEFUL FOR:	I AM GRATEFUL FOR:	I AM GRATEFUL FOR:

Final task: schedule next week!
NOW, PUT THESE TASKS & RITUALS
IN YOUR CALENDAR.
GO FORTH AND BE AWESOME!

MARCH 2, 2023	MARCH 3, 2023	MARCH 4, 2023	MARCH 5, 2023
THURSDAY	FRIDAY	SATURDAY	SUNDAY
INTENTION:	INTENTION:	INTENTION:	INTENTION:
:	:	:	:
:	:	:	:
:	:	:	:
:	:	:	:
:	:	:	:
:	:	:	:
:	:	:	:
:	:	:	:
:	:	:	:
:	:	:	:
:	:	:	:
:	:	:	:
:	:	:	:
:	:	:	:
:	:	:	:
:	:	:	:
HOW AM I SPENDING MY ENERGY?	HOW DO I AFFECT MY WORLD?	WHAT COULD I LET GO OF?	WHAT IS WORKING WELL FOR ME?
:	:	:	:
:	:	:	:
:	:	:	:
:	:	:	:
:	:	:	:
:	:	:	:
:	:	:	:
:	:	:	:
:	:	:	:
:	:	:	:
:	:	:	:
:	:	:	:
:	:	:	:
I AM GRATEFUL FOR:	I AM GRATEFUL FOR:	I AM GRATEFUL FOR:	I AM GRATEFUL FOR:

Top 3 Goals

_____

_____

_____

Weekly Alignment

Focus

Habit Tracking

⬡ = _____

◯ = _____

▢ = _____

✿ = _____

RITUALS FOR LIVING CHALLENGE

{
THIS WEEK: BREATHE.
ONCE EACH DAY, CLOSE YOUR EYES AND TAKE
TEN FULL BREATHS, INHALING DEEPLY INTO YOUR
BELLY. LET YOUR EXHALE BE LONGER THAN
YOUR INHALE.
}

Rituals For Thriving

- EXERCISE
- MEDITATE / BREATHE
- JOURNAL
- DANCE
- GO ON A DATE
- CONNECT WITH NATURE
- VISUALIZE
- FAMILY TIME
- COOK / EAT A HEALTHY MEAL
- ORGANIZE MY SPACE / LIFE
- GET RID OF THINGS I DON'T LO
- BE WITH FRIENDS
- PLAY
- LET GO / FORGIVE
- SING / MAKE MUSIC
- CREATE ART
- READ FOR ENJOYMENT
- CONNECT / PRAY
- CALL SOMEONE / WRITE A LET
- STRETCH / DO YOGA
- MASSAGE / EXCHANGE TOUCH
- SERVE MY COMMUNITY
- TECHNOLOGY BREAK

Wins from last week (what I gained / how I grew)

_____

_____

_____

How will I reframe something I find difficult, painful, or stressful?

_____

_____

_____

How will I create more freedom in my life this week?

_____

_____

Capture Your Brilliance - Dream, Expand, Record, Reflect:

The mind follows the breath. Deepen your breath to calm your mind.

- The Well Life Book

Tasks

- MONTHLY PLAN
- INCOMPLETE FROM LAST WEEK
- LIFE DUTIES
- ★ STAR THE MOST IMPORTANT TASKS

MARCH 6, 2023	MARCH 7, 2023	MARCH 8, 2023
MONDAY	TUESDAY ◯	WEDNESDAY
INTENTION:	INTENTION:	INTENTION:
:	:	:
:	:	:
:	:	:
:	:	:
:	:	:
:	:	:
:	:	:
:	:	:
:	:	:
:	:	:
:	:	:
:	:	:
:	:	:
:	:	:
:	:	:
WHAT SHALL I BE FOCUSED ON?	WHERE IS MY ATTENTION GOING?	WHAT PERSPECTIVE DO I CHOOSE?
:	:	:
:	:	:
:	:	:
:	:	:
:	:	:
:	:	:
:	:	:
:	:	:
:	:	:
:	:	:
:	:	:
:	:	:
I AM GRATEFUL FOR:	I AM GRATEFUL FOR:	I AM GRATEFUL FOR:

Final task: schedule next week!
NOW, PUT THESE TASKS & RITUALS
IN YOUR CALENDAR,
GO FORTH AND BE AWESOME!

MARCH 9, 2023	MARCH 10, 2023	MARCH 11, 2023	MARCH 12, 2023
THURSDAY	FRIDAY	SATURDAY	SUNDAY
INTENTION:	INTENTION:	INTENTION:	INTENTION:

:	:	:	:
:	:	:	:
:	:	:	:
:	:	:	:
:	:	:	:
:	:	:	:
:	:	:	:
:	:	:	:
:	:	:	:
:	:	:	:
:	:	:	:
:	:	:	:
:	:	:	:
:	:	:	:
:	:	:	:
:	:	:	:

HOW AM I SPENDING MY ENERGY?	HOW DO I AFFECT MY WORLD?	WHAT COULD I LET GO OF?	WHAT IS WORKING WELL FOR ME?
:	:	:	:
:	:	:	:
:	:	:	:
:	:	:	:
:	:	:	:
:	:	:	:
:	:	:	:
:	:	:	:
:	:	:	:
:	:	:	:
:	:	:	:
:	:	:	:
:	:	:	:

I AM GRATEFUL FOR:	I AM GRATEFUL FOR:	I AM GRATEFUL FOR:	I AM GRATEFUL FOR:

Top 3 Goals

_____

_____

_____

Weekly Alignment

Focus

Habit Tracking

◯ = _____

◯ = _____

▢ = _____

✾ = _____

Rituals For Thriving

- ○ EXERCISE
- ○ MEDITATE / BREATHE
- ○ JOURNAL
- ○ DANCE
- ○ GO ON A DATE
- ○ CONNECT WITH NATURE
- ○ VISUALIZE
- ○ FAMILY TIME
- ○ COOK / EAT A HEALTHY MEAL
- ○ ORGANIZE MY SPACE / LIFE
- ○ GET RID OF THINGS I DON'T LOV
- ○ BE WITH FRIENDS
- ○ PLAY
- ○ LET GO / FORGIVE
- ○ SING / MAKE MUSIC
- ○ CREATE ART
- ○ READ FOR ENJOYMENT
- ○ CONNECT / PRAY
- ○ CALL SOMEONE / WRITE A LET
- ○ STRETCH / DO YOGA
- ○ MASSAGE / EXCHANGE TOUCH
- ○ SERVE MY COMMUNITY
- ○ TECHNOLOGY BREAK

RITUALS FOR LIVING CHALLENGE

{ THIS WEEK, FEED YOUR BODY GOOD THINGS. EACH DAY REPLACE ONE NOT-SO-HEALTHY THING WITH A HEALTHY THING. IF YOU ALREADY DO THIS, EACH DAY TRY A NEW FRUIT, VEGETABLE, OR SPICE. IF THERE AREN'T ANY YOU HAVEN'T TRIED, TRY A NEW RECIPE. }

Wins from last week (what I gained / how I grew)

_____

_____

_____

How will I reframe something I find difficult, painful, or stressful?

_____

_____

_____

How will I create more freedom in my life this week?

_____

_____

Capture Your Brilliance - Dream, Expand, Record, Reflect:

Tasks

- MONTHLY PLAN
- INCOMPLETE FROM LAST WEEK
- LIFE DUTIES
- ★ STAR THE MOST IMPORTANT TASKS

MARCH 13, 2023	MARCH 14, 2023	MARCH 15, 2023
MONDAY	TUESDAY ◑	WEDNESDAY
INTENTION:	INTENTION:	INTENTION:
:	:	:
:	:	:
:	:	:
:	:	:
:	:	:
:	:	:
:	:	:
:	:	:
:	:	:
:	:	:
:	:	:
:	:	:
:	:	:
:	:	:
:	:	:
WHAT SHALL I BE FOCUSED ON?	WHERE IS MY ATTENTION GOING?	WHAT PERSPECTIVE DO I CHOOSE?
:	:	:
:	:	:
:	:	:
:	:	:
:	:	:
:	:	:
:	:	:
:	:	:
:	:	:
:	:	:
:	:	:
:	:	:
:	:	:
I AM GRATEFUL FOR:	I AM GRATEFUL FOR:	I AM GRATEFUL FOR:

Final task: schedule next week!
NOW, PUT THESE TASKS & RITUALS
IN YOUR CALENDAR.
GO FORTH AND BE AWESOME!

MARCH 16, 2023	MARCH 17, 2023	MARCH 18, 2023	MARCH 19, 2023
THURSDAY	FRIDAY	SATURDAY	SUNDAY
INTENTION:	INTENTION:	INTENTION:	INTENTION:

:	:	:	:
:	:	:	:
:	:	:	:
:	:	:	:
:	:	:	:
:	:	:	:
:	:	:	:
:	:	:	:
:	:	:	:
:	:	:	:
:	:	:	:
:	:	:	:
:	:	:	:
:	:	:	:
:	:	:	:

HOW AM I SPENDING MY ENERGY?	HOW DO I AFFECT MY WORLD?	WHAT COULD I LET GO OF?	WHAT IS WORKING WELL FOR ME?
:	:	:	:
:	:	:	:
:	:	:	:
:	:	:	:
:	:	:	:
:	:	:	:
:	:	:	:
:	:	:	:
:	:	:	:
:	:	:	:
:	:	:	:
:	:	:	:

I AM GRATEFUL FOR:	I AM GRATEFUL FOR:	I AM GRATEFUL FOR:	I AM GRATEFUL FOR:

Top 3 Goals

_____

_____

_____

Weekly Alignment

Focus

Habit Tracking

⬡ = _____

◯ = _____

▢ = _____

✦ = _____

Rituals For Thriving

○ EXERCISE
○ MEDITATE / BREATHE
○ JOURNAL
○ DANCE
○ GO ON A DATE
○ CONNECT WITH NATURE
○ VISUALIZE
○ FAMILY TIME
○ COOK / EAT A HEALTHY MEAL
○ ORGANIZE MY SPACE / LIFE
○ GET RID OF THINGS I DON'T LOV
○ BE WITH FRIENDS
○ PLAY
○ LET GO / FORGIVE
○ SING / MAKE MUSIC
○ CREATE ART
○ READ FOR ENJOYMENT
○ CONNECT / PRAY
○ CALL SOMEONE / WRITE A LET
○ STRETCH / DO YOGA
○ MASSAGE / EXCHANGE TOUCH
○ SERVE MY COMMUNITY
○ TECHNOLOGY BREAK

RITUALS FOR LIVING CHALLENGE

{ THIS WEEK, MAKE UP A SONG OR POEM. IF THIS IS NOT SOMETHING YOU'D NORMALLY DO, THINK OF IT AS AN EXERCISE THAT CHALLENGES THE WIRING OF YOUR BRAIN AND STRETCHES YOUR COMFORT ZONE. IF YOU ARE BRAVE ENOUGH, SHARE IT WITH SOMEONE. }

Wins from last week (what I gained / how I grew)

_____

_____

_____

How will I reframe something I find difficult, painful, or stressful?

_____

_____

_____

How will I create more freedom in my life this week?

_____

_____

Capture Your Brilliance - Dream, Expand, Record, Reflect:

You don't need to be prepared for every possible obstacle before you start.
- The Well Life Book

Tasks

- MONTHLY PLAN
- INCOMPLETE FROM LAST WEEK
- LIFE DUTIES
- ★ STAR THE MOST IMPORTANT TASKS

MARCH 20, 2023	MARCH 21, 2023	MARCH 22, 2023
MONDAY	TUESDAY ●	WEDNESDAY
INTENTION:	INTENTION:	INTENTION:
:	:	:
:	:	:
:	:	:
:	:	:
:	:	:
:	:	:
:	:	:
:	:	:
:	:	:
:	:	:
:	:	:
:	:	:
:	:	:
:	:	:
:	:	:
:	:	
WHAT SHALL I BE FOCUSED ON?	WHERE IS MY ATTENTION GOING?	WHAT PERSPECTIVE DO I CHOOSE?
:	:	:
:	:	:
:	:	:
:	:	:
:	:	:
:	:	:
:	:	:
:	:	:
:	:	:
:	:	:
:	:	:
:	:	:
I AM GRATEFUL FOR:	I AM GRATEFUL FOR:	I AM GRATEFUL FOR:

Final task: schedule next week!
NOW, PUT THESE TASKS & RITUALS
IN YOUR CALENDAR.
GO FORTH AND BE AWESOME!

MARCH 23, 2023	MARCH 24, 2023	MARCH 25, 2023	MARCH 26, 2023
THURSDAY	FRIDAY	SATURDAY	SUNDAY
INTENTION:	INTENTION:	INTENTION:	INTENTION:

:	:	:	:
:	:	:	:
:	:	:	:
:	:	:	:
:	:	:	:
:	:	:	:
:	:	:	:
:	:	:	:
:	:	:	:
:	:	:	:
:	:	:	:
:	:	:	:
:	:	:	:
:	:	:	:
:	:	:	:

HOW AM I SPENDING MY ENERGY?	HOW DO I AFFECT MY WORLD?	WHAT COULD I LET GO OF?	WHAT IS WORKING WELL FOR ME?
:	:	:	:
:	:	:	:
:	:	:	:
:	:	:	:
:	:	:	:
:	:	:	:
:	:	:	:
:	:	:	:
:	:	:	:
:	:	:	:
:	:	:	:

I AM GRATEFUL FOR:	I AM GRATEFUL FOR:	I AM GRATEFUL FOR:	I AM GRATEFUL FOR:

Life Edits

It's time to reflect on the past quarter, and decide what you want to refine as you move forward.

1. What was your biggest time and/or energy waster in the past quarter?

_____

2. Which activities and rituals yielded the biggest "return" for you (tangible or intangible) in the past quarter?

_____

_____

3. Review the habits you've been tracking in the last quarter. Reflect on the progress you've made and the habits you want to continue to work on as you move forward.

_____

_____

4. Is there anything you've been procrastinating over the past quarter?

_____

_____

5. What has been infringing on your happiness, health, or productivity in the past quarter that you intend to let go of in the coming quarter?

_____

_____

6. Self-Trust Personal Assessment: Compare your self-trust to the start of the year and see how you're doing. Rate your ability to trust yourself in each of the following areas of life on a scale of 0 to 10.

(Total lack of trust ⓪ ･･･････ ⑩ Complete trust)

COMMUNICATION: How much do you trust yourself to tell the truth, say what needs to be said for healthy relationships, speak kindly, & express yourself authentically? _____

DEPENDABILITY: How much do you trust yourself to show up for friends and family, and support them when they need it? _____

TIME MANAGEMENT: How much do you trust yourself to be on time, to stick to your schedule and to plan appropriately? _____

FOLLOW THROUGH: How much do you trust yourself to follow through on your projects, in the time frame intended, to completion? _____

FOCUS: How much do you trust yourself to stay focused on what you have chosen to work on & avoid indulging in distraction? _____

MONEY: How much do you trust yourself to stay conscious of what you have, to maintain a positive attitude around money & to avoid taking on unnecessary debt? _____

HEALTH MAINTENANCE: How much do you trust yourself to treat your body & soul well, to get the care you need & to be kind to yourself? _____

NUTRITION: How much do you trust yourself to make good food choices, to eat in a healthy manner & to stick with your agreements around eating? _____

WORK PERFORMANCE: How much do you trust yourself to honor the work you do, to do your best & to show up enthusiastically? _____

VALUES: How much do you trust yourself to live by your core values? _____

Quarter Two Breakdown

1. Get into your *ritual for planning* space. Do whatever you do to tune in (light a candle, take a breath, go to a peaceful spot, set an intention, etc.).

2. Look back at your What I Will Accomplish This Year list, and find all the projects that will be occurring in the coming quarter. Write each one in the table below and mark the appropriate month number(s) for the month(s) in which it will taking place.

Project	Month		
	Apr	May	Jun
	①	②	③
	①	②	③
	①	②	③
	①	②	③
	①	②	③
	①	②	③
	①	②	③
	①	②	③
	①	②	③
	①	②	③
	①	②	③
	①	②	③
	①	②	③
	①	②	③
	①	②	③
	①	②	③
	①	②	③
	①	②	③
	①	②	③
	①	②	③
	①	②	③
	①	②	③
	①	②	③

April
Project Breakdown

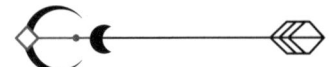

1. Get into your *ritual for planning* space.

2. Gather the projects from the Quarterly Breakdown that pertain to this month and write each one on a PROJECT line below.

3. Under the project name, enter all of the tasks that are involved in the project. Each of these tasks must be a single action step so that it can be put into your calendar and when you see it, no analysis needs to occur – you know exactly what to do.

_____
PROJECT

_____   _____

_____   _____

_____   _____

_____   _____

_____   _____

_____   _____

_____
PROJECT

_____   _____

_____   _____

_____   _____

_____   _____

_____   _____

_____   _____

PROJECT

PROJECT

PROJECT

May
Project Breakdown

1. Get into your *ritual for planning* space.

2. Gather the projects from the Quarterly Breakdown that pertain to this month and write each one on a PROJECT line below.

3. Under the project name, enter all of the tasks that are involved in the project. Each of these tasks must be a single action step so that it can be put into your calendar and when you see it, no analysis needs to occur – you know exactly what to do.

_____
PROJECT

_____   _____

_____   _____

_____   _____

_____   _____

_____   _____

_____   _____

_____   _____

_____
PROJECT

_____   _____

_____   _____

_____   _____

_____   _____

_____   _____

_____   _____

PROJECT

_____   _____
_____   _____
_____   _____
_____   _____
_____   _____
_____   _____
_____   _____

PROJECT

_____   _____
_____   _____
_____   _____
_____   _____
_____   _____
_____   _____
_____   _____

PROJECT

_____   _____
_____   _____
_____   _____
_____   _____
_____   _____
_____   _____
_____   _____

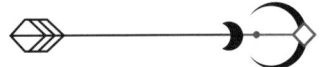
June
Project Breakdown

1. Get into your *ritual for planning* space.

2. Gather the projects from the Quarterly Breakdown that pertain to this month and write each one on a PROJECT line below.

3. Under the project name, enter all of the tasks that are involved in the project. Each of these tasks must be a single action step so that it can be put into your calendar and when you see it, no analysis needs to occur – you know exactly what to do.

PROJECT

PROJECT

PROJECT

PROJECT

PROJECT

APRIL

Monday	Tuesday	Wednesday
(27)	(28)	(29)
3	4	5
10	11	12
17	18	19
24	25 ANZAC Day	26

Notes:

Thursday	Friday	Saturday	Sunday
(30)	(31)	1 April Fool's Day	2
6 ○	7 Good Friday	8	9 Easter
13 ◑	14	15	16
20 ♉ Taurus ●	21	22 Earth Day Eid Al-Fitr Begins	23
27 Freedom Day (SA) ◐	28 Arbor Day	29	30

●: New Moon ◐: First Quarter ○: Full Moon ◑: Third Quarter

Dates for moon phases are based on the Eastern Time Zone of the United States. In other parts of the world these phases may technically occur on the previous or following day. If precision is a concern, we encourage you to consult a moon phase calendar specific to your time zone.

121

MARCH 27 – APRIL 2, 2023

Top 3 Goals

_____

_____

_____

Weekly Alignment

Focus

Habit Tracking

◯ = _____

◯ = _____

▢ = _____

✧ = _____

RITUALS FOR LIVING CHALLENGE

{ THIS WEEK, TRY TO MAKE SOMEONE LAUGH EACH DAY. IF YOU DON'T KNOW ANY JOKES, FIND SOME GOOD ONES ONLINE, OR EMPLOY OTHER METHODS, SUCH AS TICKLING OR DOING A FUNNY DANCE. LAUGHTER IS MEDICINE. }

Rituals For Thriving

- ○ EXERCISE
- ○ MEDITATE / BREATHE
- ○ JOURNAL
- ○ DANCE
- ○ GO ON A DATE
- ○ CONNECT WITH NATURE
- ○ VISUALIZE
- ○ FAMILY TIME
- ○ COOK / EAT A HEALTHY MEAL
- ○ ORGANIZE MY SPACE / LIFE
- ○ GET RID OF THINGS I DON'T LOVE
- ○ BE WITH FRIENDS
- ○ PLAY
- ○ LET GO / FORGIVE
- ○ SING / MAKE MUSIC
- ○ CREATE ART
- ○ READ FOR ENJOYMENT
- ○ CONNECT / PRAY
- ○ CALL SOMEONE / WRITE A LETTER
- ○ STRETCH / DO YOGA
- ○ MASSAGE / EXCHANGE TOUCH
- ○ SERVE MY COMMUNITY
- ○ TECHNOLOGY BREAK

Wins from last week (what I gained / how I grew)

_____
_____
_____

How will I reframe something I find difficult, painful, or stressful?

_____
_____
_____

How will I create more freedom in my life this week?

_____
_____

Capture Your Brilliance - Dream, Expand, Record, Reflect:

Tasks

- MONTHLY PLAN
- INCOMPLETE FROM LAST WEEK
- LIFE DUTIES
- ★ STAR THE MOST IMPORTANT TASKS

MARCH 27, 2023	MARCH 28, 2023 ◑	MARCH 29, 2023
MONDAY	TUESDAY	WEDNESDAY
INTENTION:	INTENTION:	INTENTION:
:	:	:
:	:	:
:	:	:
:	:	:
:	:	:
:	:	:
:	:	:
:	:	:
:	:	:
:	:	:
:	:	:
:	:	:
:	:	:
:	:	:
:	:	
WHAT SHALL I BE FOCUSED ON?	WHERE IS MY ATTENTION GOING?	WHAT PERSPECTIVE DO I CHOOSE
:	:	:
:	:	:
:	:	:
:	:	:
:	:	:
:	:	:
:	:	:
:	:	:
:	:	:
:	:	:
:	:	:
:	:	:
I AM GRATEFUL FOR:	I AM GRATEFUL FOR:	I AM GRATEFUL FOR

Final task: schedule next week!

NOW, PUT THESE TASKS & RITUALS
IN YOUR CALENDAR.
GO FORTH AND BE AWESOME!

MARCH 30, 2023	MARCH 31, 2023	APRIL 1, 2023	APRIL 2, 2023
THURSDAY	FRIDAY	SATURDAY	SUNDAY
INTENTION:	INTENTION:	INTENTION:	INTENTION:
:	:	:	:
:	:	:	:
:	:	:	:
:	:	:	:
:	:	:	:
:	:	:	:
:	:	:	:
:	:	:	:
:	:	:	:
:	:	:	:
:	:	:	:
:	:	:	:
:	:	:	:
:	:	:	:
:	:	:	:
HOW AM I SPENDING MY ENERGY?	HOW DO I AFFECT MY WORLD?	WHAT COULD I LET GO OF?	WHAT IS WORKING WELL FOR ME?
:	:	:	:
:	:	:	:
:	:	:	:
:	:	:	:
:	:	:	:
:	:	:	:
:	:	:	:
:	:	:	:
:	:	:	:
:	:	:	:
:	:	:	:
:	:	:	:
:	:	:	:
I AM GRATEFUL FOR:	I AM GRATEFUL FOR:	I AM GRATEFUL FOR:	I AM GRATEFUL FOR:

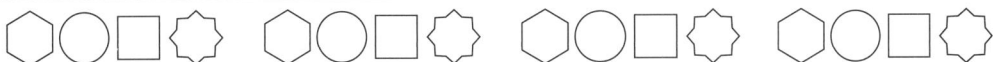

Top 3 Goals

_____

_____

_____

Weekly Alignment

Focus

Rituals For Thriving

- ○ EXERCISE
- ○ MEDITATE / BREATHE
- ○ JOURNAL
- ○ DANCE
- ○ GO ON A DATE
- ○ CONNECT WITH NATURE
- ○ VISUALIZE
- ○ FAMILY TIME
- ○ COOK / EAT A HEALTHY MEAL
- ○ ORGANIZE MY SPACE / LIFE
- ○ GET RID OF THINGS I DON'T LOVE
- ○ BE WITH FRIENDS
- ○ PLAY
- ○ LET GO / FORGIVE
- ○ SING / MAKE MUSIC
- ○ CREATE ART
- ○ READ FOR ENJOYMENT
- ○ CONNECT / PRAY
- ○ CALL SOMEONE / WRITE A LETTER
- ○ STRETCH / DO YOGA
- ○ MASSAGE / EXCHANGE TOUCH
- ○ SERVE MY COMMUNITY
- ○ TECHNOLOGY BREAK

Habit Tracking

⬡ = _____

◯ = _____

☐ = _____

✧ = _____

RITUALS FOR LIVING CHALLENGE

{ THIS WEEK, DANCE ON AT LEAST THREE SEPARATE OCCASIONS. IT DOESN'T MATTER WHETHER YOU LOOK GOOD OR HAVE ANY SKILL. DANCE IS SUCH A BASIC, PRIMAL FORM OF EXPRESSION, RITUAL, & RELEASE. JUST PUT ON MUSIC YOU LOVE AND LET YOUR BODY MOVE. }

Wins from last week (what I gained / how I grew)

_____

_____

_____

How will I reframe something I find difficult, painful, or stressful?

_____

_____

_____

How will I create more freedom in my life this week?

_____

_____

Capture Your Brilliance - Dream, Expand, Record, Reflect:

The base state of every human's consciousness is love.

- The Well Life Book

Tasks

- MONTHLY PLAN
- INCOMPLETE FROM LAST WEEK
- LIFE DUTIES
- ★ STAR THE MOST IMPORTANT TASKS

APRIL 3, 2023	APRIL 4, 2023	APRIL 5, 2023
MONDAY	TUESDAY	WEDNESDAY
INTENTION:	INTENTION:	INTENTION:
:	:	:
:	:	:
:	:	:
:	:	:
:	:	:
:	:	:
:	:	:
:	:	:
:	:	:
:	:	:
:	:	:
:	:	:
:	:	:
:	:	:
WHAT SHALL I BE FOCUSED ON?	WHERE IS MY ATTENTION GOING?	WHAT PERSPECTIVE DO I CHOOSE?
:	:	:
:	:	:
:	:	:
:	:	:
:	:	:
:	:	:
:	:	:
:	:	:
:	:	:
:	:	:
:	:	:
:	:	:
:	:	:
I AM GRATEFUL FOR:	I AM GRATEFUL FOR:	I AM GRATEFUL FOR:

Final task: schedule next week!
NOW, PUT THESE TASKS & RITUALS
IN YOUR CALENDAR.
GO FORTH AND BE AWESOME!

APRIL 6, 2023	APRIL 7, 2023	APRIL 8, 2023	APRIL 9, 2023
THURSDAY ○	FRIDAY	SATURDAY	SUNDAY
INTENTION:	INTENTION:	INTENTION:	INTENTION:
:	:	:	:
:	:	:	:
:	:	:	:
:	:	:	:
:	:	:	:
:	:	:	:
:	:	:	:
:	:	:	:
:	:	:	:
:	:	:	:
:	:	:	:
:	:	:	:
:	:	:	:
:	:	:	:
:	:	:	:
:	:	:	:
:	:	:	:
HOW AM I SPENDING MY ENERGY?	HOW DO I AFFECT MY WORLD?	WHAT COULD I LET GO OF?	WHAT IS WORKING WELL FOR ME?
:	:	:	:
:	:	:	:
:	:	:	:
:	:	:	:
:	:	:	:
:	:	:	:
:	:	:	:
:	:	:	:
:	:	:	:
:	:	:	:
:	:	:	:
:	:	:	:
:	:	:	:
I AM GRATEFUL FOR:	I AM GRATEFUL FOR:	I AM GRATEFUL FOR:	I AM GRATEFUL FOR:

Top 3 Goals

Weekly Alignment

Focus

Habit Tracking

⬡ = _____

◯ = _____

▢ = _____

✦ = _____

Rituals For Thriving

- ○ EXERCISE
- ○ MEDITATE / BREATHE
- ○ JOURNAL
- ○ DANCE
- ○ GO ON A DATE
- ○ CONNECT WITH NATURE
- ○ VISUALIZE
- ○ FAMILY TIME
- ○ COOK / EAT A HEALTHY MEAL
- ○ ORGANIZE MY SPACE / LIFE
- ○ GET RID OF THINGS I DON'T LOVE
- ○ BE WITH FRIENDS
- ○ PLAY
- ○ LET GO / FORGIVE
- ○ SING / MAKE MUSIC
- ○ CREATE ART
- ○ READ FOR ENJOYMENT
- ○ CONNECT / PRAY
- ○ CALL SOMEONE / WRITE A LETTER
- ○ STRETCH / DO YOGA
- ○ MASSAGE / EXCHANGE TOUCH
- ○ SERVE MY COMMUNITY
- ○ TECHNOLOGY BREAK

RITUALS FOR LIVING CHALLENGE

{ PUT YOUR HANDS AND/OR BARE FEET DIRECTLY ON THE EARTH EACH DAY. THIS IS YOUR HOME. THIS IS THE SOIL THAT SUSTAINS OUR PLANTS AND ANIMALS. FEEL GROUNDED & CONNECTED. EXTRA CREDIT: CONNECT AWAY FROM CIVILIZATION OR SLEEP ON THE GROUND. }

Wins from last week (what I gained / how I grew)

_____

_____

How will I reframe something I find difficult, painful, or stressful?

_____

_____

How will I create more freedom in my life this week?

_____

_____

Capture Your Brilliance - Dream, Expand, Record, Reflect:

Tasks

- MONTHLY PLAN
- INCOMPLETE FROM LAST WEEK
- LIFE DUTIES
- ★ STAR THE MOST IMPORTANT TASKS

APRIL 10, 2023	APRIL 11, 2023	APRIL 12, 2023
MONDAY	TUESDAY	WEDNESDAY
INTENTION:	INTENTION:	INTENTION:
:	:	:
:	:	:
:	:	:
:	:	:
:	:	:
:	:	:
:	:	:
:	:	:
:	:	:
:	:	:
:	:	:
:	:	:
:	:	:
:	:	:
:	:	:
:	:	:
WHAT SHALL I BE FOCUSED ON?	WHERE IS MY ATTENTION GOING?	WHAT PERSPECTIVE DO I CHOOSE?
:	:	:
:	:	:
:	:	:
:	:	:
:	:	:
:	:	:
:	:	:
:	:	:
:	:	:
:	:	:
:	:	:
:	:	:
I AM GRATEFUL FOR:	I AM GRATEFUL FOR:	I AM GRATEFUL FOR:

Final task: schedule next week!
NOW, PUT THESE TASKS & RITUALS
IN YOUR CALENDAR.
GO FORTH AND BE AWESOME!

APRIL 13, 2023	APRIL 14, 2023	APRIL 15, 2023	APRIL 16, 2023
THURSDAY ◑	FRIDAY	SATURDAY	SUNDAY
INTENTION:	INTENTION:	INTENTION:	INTENTION:
:	:	:	:
:	:	:	:
:	:	:	:
:	:	:	:
:	:	:	:
:	:	:	:
:	:	:	:
:	:	:	:
:	:	:	:
:	:	:	:
:	:	:	:
:	:	:	:
:	:	:	:
:	:	:	:
:	:	:	:
HOW AM I SPENDING MY ENERGY?	HOW DO I AFFECT MY WORLD?	WHAT COULD I LET GO OF?	WHAT IS WORKING WELL FOR ME?
:	:	:	:
:	:	:	:
:	:	:	:
:	:	:	:
:	:	:	:
:	:	:	:
:	:	:	:
:	:	:	:
:	:	:	:
:	:	:	:
:	:	:	:
:	:	:	:
I AM GRATEFUL FOR:	I AM GRATEFUL FOR:	I AM GRATEFUL FOR:	I AM GRATEFUL FOR:

Top 3 Goals

_____

_____

_____

Weekly Alignment

Focus

Rituals For Thriving

- ○ EXERCISE
- ○ MEDITATE / BREATHE
- ○ JOURNAL
- ○ DANCE
- ○ GO ON A DATE
- ○ CONNECT WITH NATURE
- ○ VISUALIZE
- ○ FAMILY TIME
- ○ COOK / EAT A HEALTHY MEAL
- ○ ORGANIZE MY SPACE / LIFE
- ○ GET RID OF THINGS I DON'T LOVE
- ○ BE WITH FRIENDS
- ○ PLAY
- ○ LET GO / FORGIVE
- ○ SING / MAKE MUSIC
- ○ CREATE ART
- ○ READ FOR ENJOYMENT
- ○ CONNECT / PRAY
- ○ CALL SOMEONE / WRITE A LETTER
- ○ STRETCH / DO YOGA
- ○ MASSAGE / EXCHANGE TOUCH
- ○ SERVE MY COMMUNITY
- ○ TECHNOLOGY BREAK

Habit Tracking

⬡ = _____

◯ = _____

▢ = _____

✦ = _____

RITUALS FOR LIVING CHALLENGE

{ THIS WEEK, CLEAN SOMETHING THAT HAS BEEN NEEDING TO BE CLEANED. IF THERE IS NOTHING IN YOUR OWN SPACE THAT NEEDS CLEANING, FIND SOMETHING OUTSIDE – SOME TRASH, SOME GRAFFITI, ETC. HONOR YOUR ENVIRONMENT. }

Wins from last week (what I gained / how I grew)

_____

_____

_____

How will I reframe something I find difficult, painful, or stressful?

_____

_____

_____

How will I create more freedom in my life this week?

_____

_____

Capture Your Brilliance - Dream, Expand, Record, Reflect:

Don't limit your success by avoiding decisions.
- The Well Life Book

Tasks

- MONTHLY PLAN
- INCOMPLETE FROM LAST WEEK
- LIFE DUTIES
- ★ STAR THE MOST IMPORTANT TASKS

APRIL 17, 2023	APRIL 18, 2023	APRIL 19, 2023
MONDAY	TUESDAY	WEDNESDAY
INTENTION:	INTENTION:	INTENTION:
:	:	:
:	:	:
:	:	:
:	:	:
:	:	:
:	:	:
:	:	:
:	:	:
:	:	:
:	:	:
:	:	:
:	:	:
:	:	:
:	:	:
WHAT SHALL I BE FOCUSED ON?	WHERE IS MY ATTENTION GOING?	WHAT PERSPECTIVE DO I CHOOSE?
:	:	:
:	:	:
:	:	:
:	:	:
:	:	:
:	:	:
:	:	:
:	:	:
:	:	:
:	:	:
:	:	:
:	:	:
I AM GRATEFUL FOR:	I AM GRATEFUL FOR:	I AM GRATEFUL FOR:

Final task: schedule next week!
NOW, PUT THESE TASKS & RITUALS
IN YOUR CALENDAR.
GO FORTH AND BE AWESOME!

APRIL 20, 2023	APRIL 21, 2023	APRIL 22, 2023	APRIL 23, 2023
THURSDAY ●	FRIDAY	SATURDAY	SUNDAY
INTENTION:	INTENTION:	INTENTION:	INTENTION:
:	:	:	:
:	:	:	:
:	:	:	:
:	:	:	:
:	:	:	:
:	:	:	:
:	:	:	:
:	:	:	:
:	:	:	:
:	:	:	:
:	:	:	:
:	:	:	:
:	:	:	:
:	:	:	:
:	:	:	:
:	:	:	:
HOW AM I SPENDING MY ENERGY?	HOW DO I AFFECT MY WORLD?	WHAT COULD I LET GO OF?	WHAT IS WORKING WELL FOR ME?
:	:	:	:
:	:	:	:
:	:	:	:
:	:	:	:
:	:	:	:
:	:	:	:
:	:	:	:
:	:	:	:
:	:	:	:
:	:	:	:
:	:	:	:
:	:	:	:
:	:	:	:
I AM GRATEFUL FOR:	I AM GRATEFUL FOR:	I AM GRATEFUL FOR:	I AM GRATEFUL FOR:

Top 3 Goals

_____

_____

_____

Weekly Alignment

Focus

Rituals For Thriving

- o EXERCISE
- o MEDITATE / BREATHE
- o JOURNAL
- o DANCE
- o GO ON A DATE
- o CONNECT WITH NATURE
- o VISUALIZE
- o FAMILY TIME
- o COOK / EAT A HEALTHY MEAL
- o ORGANIZE MY SPACE / LIFE
- o GET RID OF THINGS I DON'T LOV
- o BE WITH FRIENDS
- o PLAY
- o LET GO / FORGIVE
- o SING / MAKE MUSIC
- o CREATE ART
- o READ FOR ENJOYMENT
- o CONNECT / PRAY
- o CALL SOMEONE / WRITE A LET
- o STRETCH / DO YOGA
- o MASSAGE / EXCHANGE TOUCH
- o SERVE MY COMMUNITY
- o TECHNOLOGY BREAK

Habit Tracking

⬡ = _____

◯ = _____

▢ = _____

✸ = _____

RITUALS FOR LIVING CHALLENGE

{ EVERY DAY, FORGIVE YOURSELF FOR EVERYTHING. CATCH YOURSELF THINKING YOU SHOULD BE DIFFERENT OR BETTER, YOUR PAST SHOULD BE DIFFERENT, OR YOU SHOULD BE MORE LIKE YOUR IDEA OF THE PERFECT HUMAN. FORGIVE YOURSELF, OVER AND OVER. }

Wins from last week (what I gained / how I grew)

_____
_____
_____

How will I reframe something I find difficult, painful, or stressful?

_____
_____
_____

How will I create more freedom in my life this week?

_____
_____

Capture Your Brilliance - Dream, Expand, Record, Reflect:

Tasks

- MONTHLY PLAN
- INCOMPLETE FROM LAST WEEK
- LIFE DUTIES
- ★ STAR THE MOST IMPORTANT TASKS

APRIL 24, 2023	APRIL 25, 2023	APRIL 26, 2023
MONDAY	TUESDAY	WEDNESDAY
INTENTION:	INTENTION:	INTENTION:
:	:	:
:	:	:
:	:	:
:	:	:
:	:	:
:	:	:
:	:	:
:	:	:
:	:	:
:	:	:
:	:	:
:	:	:
:	:	:
:	:	:
:	:	:
:	:	:
WHAT SHALL I BE FOCUSED ON?	WHERE IS MY ATTENTION GOING?	WHAT PERSPECTIVE DO I CHOOSE?
:	:	:
:	:	:
:	:	:
:	:	:
:	:	:
:	:	:
:	:	:
:	:	:
:	:	:
:	:	:
:	:	:
:	:	:
I AM GRATEFUL FOR:	I AM GRATEFUL FOR:	I AM GRATEFUL FOR:

Final task: schedule next week!
NOW, PUT THESE TASKS & RITUALS
IN YOUR CALENDAR.
GO FORTH AND BE AWESOME!

APRIL 27, 2023	APRIL 28, 2023	APRIL 29, 2023	APRIL 30, 2023
THURSDAY	FRIDAY	SATURDAY	SUNDAY
INTENTION:	INTENTION:	INTENTION:	INTENTION:
:	:	:	:
:	:	:	:
:	:	:	:
:	:	:	:
:	:	:	:
:	:	:	:
:	:	:	:
:	:	:	:
:	:	:	:
:	:	:	:
:	:	:	:
:	:	:	:
:	:	:	:
:	:	:	:
:	:	:	:
HOW AM I SPENDING MY ENERGY?	HOW DO I AFFECT MY WORLD?	WHAT COULD I LET GO OF?	WHAT IS WORKING WELL FOR ME?
:	:	:	:
:	:	:	:
:	:	:	:
:	:	:	:
:	:	:	:
:	:	:	:
:	:	:	:
:	:	:	:
:	:	:	:
:	:	:	:
:	:	:	:
:	:	:	:
:	:	:	:
I AM GRATEFUL FOR:	I AM GRATEFUL FOR:	I AM GRATEFUL FOR:	I AM GRATEFUL FOR:

MAY

Monday	Tuesday	Wednesday
1 May Day	2	3
8	9	10
15	16	17
22	23	24
29 Memorial Day	30	31

Notes:

Thursday	Friday	Saturday	Sunday
4	5 Cinco de Mayo ○	6	7
11	12 ◐	13	14 Mother's Day
18	19 ●	20	21 ♓ Gemini
25 Shavuot Begins	26	27 ◐	28
(1)	(2)	(3)	(4)

●: New Moon ◐: First Quarter ○: Full Moon ◑: Third Quarter

ates for moon phases are based on the Eastern Time Zone of the United States. In other parts of the world these phases may technically ur on the previous or following day. If precision is a concern, we encourage you to consult a moon phase calendar specific to your time zone.

Top 3 Goals

Weekly Alignment

Focus

Habit Tracking

⬡ = _____

◯ = _____

▢ = _____

⬖ = _____

RITUALS FOR LIVING CHALLENGE

{ THIS WEEK, REDUCE YOUR SCREEN TIME. INSTEAD OF TURNING CONSTANTLY TO YOUR CELL PHONE, TELEVISION, TABLET, AND COMPUTER, FIND OTHER WAYS TO BE AMUSED. BE SATISFIED WITH SILENCE AND NATURAL OBJECTS. }

Rituals For Thriving

- o EXERCISE
- o MEDITATE / BREATHE
- o JOURNAL
- o DANCE
- o GO ON A DATE
- o CONNECT WITH NATURE
- o VISUALIZE
- o FAMILY TIME
- o COOK / EAT A HEALTHY MEAL
- o ORGANIZE MY SPACE / LIFE
- o GET RID OF THINGS I DON'T LO
- o BE WITH FRIENDS
- o PLAY
- o LET GO / FORGIVE
- o SING / MAKE MUSIC
- o CREATE ART
- o READ FOR ENJOYMENT
- o CONNECT / PRAY
- o CALL SOMEONE / WRITE A LET
- o STRETCH / DO YOGA
- o MASSAGE / EXCHANGE TOUCH
- o SERVE MY COMMUNITY
- o TECHNOLOGY BREAK

Wins from last week (what I gained / how I grew)

_____

_____

_____

How will I reframe something I find difficult, painful, or stressful?

_____

_____

_____

How will I create more freedom in my life this week?

_____

_____

Capture Your Brilliance - Dream, Expand, Record, Reflect:

Open up. Let the light come in and lead the way.

- The Well Life Book

Tasks

- MONTHLY PLAN
- INCOMPLETE FROM LAST WEEK
- LIFE DUTIES
- ★ STAR THE MOST IMPORTANT TASKS

MAY 1, 2023	MAY 2, 2023	MAY 3, 2023
MONDAY	TUESDAY	WEDNESDAY
INTENTION:	INTENTION:	INTENTION:
:	:	:
:	:	:
:	:	:
:	:	:
:	:	:
:	:	:
:	:	:
:	:	:
:	:	:
:	:	:
:	:	:
:	:	:
:	:	:
:	:	:
:	:	:
:	:	
WHAT SHALL I BE FOCUSED ON?	WHERE IS MY ATTENTION GOING?	WHAT PERSPECTIVE DO I CHOOSE?
:	:	:
:	:	:
:	:	:
:	:	:
:	:	:
:	:	:
:	:	:
:	:	:
:	:	:
:	:	:
:	:	:
:	:	:
I AM GRATEFUL FOR:	I AM GRATEFUL FOR:	I AM GRATEFUL FOR:

Final task: schedule next week!
NOW, PUT THESE TASKS & RITUALS
IN YOUR CALENDAR.
GO FORTH AND BE AWESOME!

MAY 4, 2023	MAY 5, 2023	MAY 6, 2023	MAY 7, 2023
THURSDAY	FRIDAY ○	SATURDAY	SUNDAY
INTENTION:	INTENTION:	INTENTION:	INTENTION:
:	:	:	:
:	:	:	:
:	:	:	:
:	:	:	:
:	:	:	:
:	:	:	:
:	:	:	:
:	:	:	:
:	:	:	:
:	:	:	:
:	:	:	:
:	:	:	:
:	:	:	:
:	:	:	:
:	:	:	:
:	:	:	:
HOW AM I SPENDING MY ENERGY?	HOW DO I AFFECT MY WORLD?	WHAT COULD I LET GO OF?	WHAT IS WORKING WELL FOR ME?
:	:	:	:
:	:	:	:
:	:	:	:
:	:	:	:
:	:	:	:
:	:	:	:
:	:	:	:
:	:	:	:
:	:	:	:
:	:	:	:
:	:	:	:
:	:	:	:
:	:	:	:
I AM GRATEFUL FOR:	I AM GRATEFUL FOR:	I AM GRATEFUL FOR:	I AM GRATEFUL FOR:

147

MAY 8 – MAY 14, 2023

Top 3 Goals

_____

_____

_____

Weekly Alignment

Focus

Habit Tracking

⬡ = _____

◯ = _____

▢ = _____

⬡ = _____

RITUALS FOR LIVING CHALLENGE

{ THIS WEEK, DO SOMETHING ADVENTUROUS. IT DOESN'T HAVE TO BE BUNGEE JUMPING. WHAT DOES ADVENTURE MEAN TO YOU? }

Rituals For Thriving

- EXERCISE
- MEDITATE / BREATHE
- JOURNAL
- DANCE
- GO ON A DATE
- CONNECT WITH NATURE
- VISUALIZE
- FAMILY TIME
- COOK / EAT A HEALTHY MEAL
- ORGANIZE MY SPACE / LIFE
- GET RID OF THINGS I DON'T LOVE
- BE WITH FRIENDS
- PLAY
- LET GO / FORGIVE
- SING / MAKE MUSIC
- CREATE ART
- READ FOR ENJOYMENT
- CONNECT / PRAY
- CALL SOMEONE / WRITE A LETTER
- STRETCH / DO YOGA
- MASSAGE / EXCHANGE TOUCH
- SERVE MY COMMUNITY
- TECHNOLOGY BREAK

Wins from last week (what I gained / how I grew)

_____
_____

How will I reframe something I find difficult, painful, or stressful?

_____
_____

How will I create more freedom in my life this week?

_____
_____

Capture Your Brilliance - Dream, Expand, Record, Reflect:

Tasks

- MONTHLY PLAN
- INCOMPLETE FROM LAST WEEK
- LIFE DUTIES
- ★ STAR THE MOST IMPORTANT TASKS

MAY 8, 2023	MAY 9, 2023	MAY 10, 2023
MONDAY	TUESDAY	WEDNESDAY
INTENTION:	INTENTION:	INTENTION:
:	:	:
:	:	:
:	:	:
:	:	:
:	:	:
:	:	:
:	:	:
:	:	:
:	:	:
:	:	:
:	:	:
:	:	:
:	:	:
:	:	:
:	:	:
WHAT SHALL I BE FOCUSED ON?	WHERE IS MY ATTENTION GOING?	WHAT PERSPECTIVE DO I CHOOSE?
:	:	:
:	:	:
:	:	:
:	:	:
:	:	:
:	:	:
:	:	:
:	:	:
:	:	:
:	:	:
:	:	:
I AM GRATEFUL FOR:	I AM GRATEFUL FOR:	I AM GRATEFUL FOR:

Final task: schedule next week!
NOW, PUT THESE TASKS & RITUALS
IN YOUR CALENDAR.
GO FORTH AND BE AWESOME!

MAY 11, 2023	MAY 12, 2023	MAY 13, 2023	MAY 14, 2023
THURSDAY	FRIDAY ◑	SATURDAY	SUNDAY
INTENTION:	INTENTION:	INTENTION:	INTENTION:
:	:	:	:
:	:	:	:
:	:	:	:
:	:	:	:
:	:	:	:
:	:	:	:
:	:	:	:
:	:	:	:
:	:	:	:
:	:	:	:
:	:	:	:
:	:	:	:
:	:	:	:
:	:	:	:
HOW AM I SPENDING MY ENERGY?	HOW DO I AFFECT MY WORLD?	WHAT COULD I LET GO OF?	WHAT IS WORKING WELL FOR ME?
:	:	:	:
:	:	:	:
:	:	:	:
:	:	:	:
:	:	:	:
:	:	:	:
:	:	:	:
:	:	:	:
:	:	:	:
:	:	:	:
:	:	:	:
:	:	:	:
I AM GRATEFUL FOR:	I AM GRATEFUL FOR:	I AM GRATEFUL FOR:	I AM GRATEFUL FOR:

Top 3 Goals

_____

_____

_____

Weekly Alignment

Focus

Rituals For Thriving

- ○ EXERCISE
- ○ MEDITATE / BREATHE
- ○ JOURNAL
- ○ DANCE
- ○ GO ON A DATE
- ○ CONNECT WITH NATURE
- ○ VISUALIZE
- ○ FAMILY TIME
- ○ COOK / EAT A HEALTHY MEAL
- ○ ORGANIZE MY SPACE / LIFE
- ○ GET RID OF THINGS I DON'T LOVE
- ○ BE WITH FRIENDS
- ○ PLAY
- ○ LET GO / FORGIVE
- ○ SING / MAKE MUSIC
- ○ CREATE ART
- ○ READ FOR ENJOYMENT
- ○ CONNECT / PRAY
- ○ CALL SOMEONE / WRITE A LETTER
- ○ STRETCH / DO YOGA
- ○ MASSAGE / EXCHANGE TOUCH
- ○ SERVE MY COMMUNITY
- ○ TECHNOLOGY BREAK

Habit Tracking

⬡ = _____

◯ = _____

▢ = _____

✦ = _____

RITUALS FOR LIVING CHALLENGE

{ CONSERVE YOUR LIFE ENERGY. USE YOUR NINJA SKILLS TO PERFORM WITH THE LEAST EXPENSE OF YOUR OWN ENERGY. BE CARING WITHOUT GIVING ENERGY AWAY. BE EFFICIENT YET UNATTACHED, CHANNEL THE AVAILABLE FORCES, CHOOSE THE PATH OF LEAST RESISTANCE. }

Wins from last week (what I gained / how I grew)

_____

_____

_____

How will I reframe something I find difficult, painful, or stressful?

_____

_____

_____

How will I create more freedom in my life this week?

_____

_____

152

Capture Your Brilliance - Dream, Expand, Record, Reflect:

Your plan is the clear path to the life of your dreams.

- The Well Life Book

Tasks

- MONTHLY PLAN
- INCOMPLETE FROM LAST WEEK
- LIFE DUTIES
- ★ STAR THE MOST IMPORTANT TASKS

MAY 15, 2023	MAY 16, 2023	MAY 17, 2023
MONDAY	TUESDAY	WEDNESDAY
INTENTION:	INTENTION:	INTENTION:
:	:	:
:	:	:
:	:	:
:	:	:
:	:	:
:	:	:
:	:	:
:	:	:
:	:	:
:	:	:
:	:	:
:	:	:
:	:	:
:	:	:
WHAT SHALL I BE FOCUSED ON?	WHERE IS MY ATTENTION GOING?	WHAT PERSPECTIVE DO I CHOOSE
:	:	:
:	:	:
:	:	:
:	:	:
:	:	:
:	:	:
:	:	:
:	:	:
:	:	:
:	:	:
:	:	:
I AM GRATEFUL FOR:	I AM GRATEFUL FOR:	I AM GRATEFUL FOR:

Final task: schedule next week!
NOW, PUT THESE TASKS & RITUALS
IN YOUR CALENDAR.
GO FORTH AND BE AWESOME!

MAY 18, 2023	MAY 19, 2023	MAY 20, 2023	MAY 21, 2023
THURSDAY	FRIDAY ●	SATURDAY	SUNDAY
INTENTION:	INTENTION:	INTENTION:	INTENTION:
:	:	:	:
:	:	:	:
:	:	:	:
:	:	:	:
:	:	:	:
:	:	:	:
:	:	:	:
:	:	:	:
:	:	:	:
:	:	:	:
:	:	:	:
:	:	:	:
:	:	:	:
:	:	:	:
HOW AM I SPENDING MY ENERGY?	HOW DO I AFFECT MY WORLD?	WHAT COULD I LET GO OF?	WHAT IS WORKING WELL FOR ME?
:	:	:	:
:	:	:	:
:	:	:	:
:	:	:	:
:	:	:	:
:	:	:	:
:	:	:	:
:	:	:	:
:	:	:	:
:	:	:	:
:	:	:	:
:	:	:	:
I AM GRATEFUL FOR:	I AM GRATEFUL FOR:	I AM GRATEFUL FOR:	I AM GRATEFUL FOR:

Top 3 Goals

_____

_____

_____

Weekly Alignment

Focus

Rituals For Thriving

- o EXERCISE
- o MEDITATE / BREATHE
- o JOURNAL
- o DANCE
- o GO ON A DATE
- o CONNECT WITH NATURE
- o VISUALIZE
- o FAMILY TIME
- o COOK / EAT A HEALTHY MEAL
- o ORGANIZE MY SPACE / LIFE
- o GET RID OF THINGS I DON'T LO
- o BE WITH FRIENDS
- o PLAY
- o LET GO / FORGIVE
- o SING / MAKE MUSIC
- o CREATE ART
- o READ FOR ENJOYMENT
- o CONNECT / PRAY
- o CALL SOMEONE / WRITE A LET
- o STRETCH / DO YOGA
- o MASSAGE / EXCHANGE TOUCH
- o SERVE MY COMMUNITY
- o TECHNOLOGY BREAK

Habit Tracking

⬡ = _____

◯ = _____

▢ = _____

✧ = _____

RITUALS FOR LIVING CHALLENGE

{ THIS WEEK, BEAUTIFY SOMETHING YOU LOOK AT ALL THE TIME. HANG A PICTURE IN YOUR BATHROOM. PUT A FRESH COAT OF PAINT ON THE WALL. FILL YOUR SPACE WITH FLOWERS. ADORN YOUR CAR WITH JEWELS. PUT A CROWN ON YOUR DOG. }

Wins from last week (what I gained / how I grew)

_____

_____

_____

How will I reframe something I find difficult, painful, or stressful?

_____

_____

_____

How will I create more freedom in my life this week?

_____

_____

Capture Your Brilliance - Dream, Expand, Record, Reflect:

Tasks

- MONTHLY PLAN
- INCOMPLETE FROM LAST WEEK
- LIFE DUTIES
- ★ STAR THE MOST IMPORTANT TASKS

MAY 22, 2023	MAY 23, 2023	MAY 24, 2023
MONDAY	TUESDAY	WEDNESDAY
INTENTION:	INTENTION:	INTENTION:
:	:	:
:	:	:
:	:	:
:	:	:
:	:	:
:	:	:
:	:	:
:	:	:
:	:	:
:	:	:
:	:	:
:	:	:
:	:	:
:	:	:
:	:	:
WHAT SHALL I BE FOCUSED ON?	WHERE IS MY ATTENTION GOING?	WHAT PERSPECTIVE DO I CHOOSE
:	:	:
:	:	:
:	:	:
:	:	:
:	:	:
:	:	:
:	:	:
:	:	:
:	:	:
:	:	:
:	:	:
:	:	:
:	:	:
I AM GRATEFUL FOR:	I AM GRATEFUL FOR:	I AM GRATEFUL FOR

Final task: schedule next week!
NOW, PUT THESE TASKS & RITUALS
IN YOUR CALENDAR.
GO FORTH AND BE AWESOME!

MAY 25, 2023	MAY 26, 2023	MAY 27, 2023	MAY 28, 2023
THURSDAY	FRIDAY	SATURDAY	SUNDAY
INTENTION:	INTENTION:	INTENTION:	INTENTION:
:	:	:	:
:	:	:	:
:	:	:	:
:	:	:	:
:	:	:	:
:	:	:	:
:	:	:	:
:	:	:	:
:	:	:	:
:	:	:	:
:	:	:	:
:	:	:	:
:	:	:	:
:	:	:	:
:	:	:	:
HOW AM I SPENDING MY ENERGY?	HOW DO I AFFECT MY WORLD?	WHAT COULD I LET GO OF?	WHAT IS WORKING WELL FOR ME?
:	:	:	:
:	:	:	:
:	:	:	:
:	:	:	:
:	:	:	:
:	:	:	:
:	:	:	:
:	:	:	:
:	:	:	:
:	:	:	:
:	:	:	:
:	:	:	:
I AM GRATEFUL FOR:	I AM GRATEFUL FOR:	I AM GRATEFUL FOR:	I AM GRATEFUL FOR:

JUNE

Monday	Tuesday	Wednesday
(29)	(30)	(31)
5	6	7
12	13	14
19 Juneteenth	20	21 Summer Solstice ♋ Cancer
26 ◐	27	28

Notes:

Thursday	Friday	Saturday	Sunday
1	2	3 ○	4
8	9	10 ◑	11
15	16	17	18 Father's Day ●
22	23	24	25
29	30	(1)	(2)

●: New Moon ◐: First Quarter ○: Full Moon ◑: Third Quarter

ates for moon phases are based on the Eastern Time Zone of the United States. In other parts of the world these phases may technically cur on the previous or following day. If precision is a concern, we encourage you to consult a moon phase calendar specific to your time zone.

Top 3 Goals

_____

_____

_____

Weekly Alignment

Focus

Rituals For Thriving

- EXERCISE
- MEDITATE / BREATHE
- JOURNAL
- DANCE
- GO ON A DATE
- CONNECT WITH NATURE
- VISUALIZE
- FAMILY TIME
- COOK / EAT A HEALTHY MEAL
- ORGANIZE MY SPACE / LIFE
- GET RID OF THINGS I DON'T LOVE
- BE WITH FRIENDS
- PLAY
- LET GO / FORGIVE
- SING / MAKE MUSIC
- CREATE ART
- READ FOR ENJOYMENT
- CONNECT / PRAY
- CALL SOMEONE / WRITE A LETTER
- STRETCH / DO YOGA
- MASSAGE / EXCHANGE TOUCH
- SERVE MY COMMUNITY
- TECHNOLOGY BREAK

Habit Tracking

◯ = _____

◯ = _____

▢ = _____

✳ = _____

RITUALS FOR LIVING CHALLENGE

{ THIS WEEK, GET SOME ART SUPPLIES, TUNE IN, AND MAKE A PIECE OF ART. IT DOESN'T MATTER IF YOU DON'T HAVE ANY TALENT. JUST CONNECT WITH WHAT'S INSIDE YOU AND LET IT OUT. WHEN IT'S DONE, FRAME IT. THEN HANG IT UP OR GIVE IT TO SOMEONE. }

Wins from last week (what I gained / how I grew)

_____

_____

How will I reframe something I find difficult, painful, or stressful?

_____

_____

How will I create more freedom in my life this week?

_____

_____

Capture Your Brilliance - Dream, Expand, Record, Reflect:

Root in authenticity, engage and feed the deepest parts of you.

- The Well Life Book

Tasks

- MONTHLY PLAN
- INCOMPLETE FROM LAST WEEK
- LIFE DUTIES
- ★ STAR THE MOST IMPORTANT TASKS

MAY 29, 2023	MAY 30, 2023	MAY 31, 2023
MONDAY	TUESDAY	WEDNESDAY
INTENTION:	INTENTION:	INTENTION:
:	:	:
:	:	:
:	:	:
:	:	:
:	:	:
:	:	:
:	:	:
:	:	:
:	:	:
:	:	:
:	:	:
:	:	:
:	:	:
:	:	:
WHAT SHALL I BE FOCUSED ON?	WHERE IS MY ATTENTION GOING?	WHAT PERSPECTIVE DO I CHOOSE
:	:	:
:	:	:
:	:	:
:	:	:
:	:	:
:	:	:
:	:	:
:	:	:
:	:	:
:	:	:
:	:	:
:	:	:
I AM GRATEFUL FOR:	I AM GRATEFUL FOR:	I AM GRATEFUL FOR:

Final task: schedule next week!
NOW, PUT THESE TASKS & RITUALS
IN YOUR CALENDAR.
GO FORTH AND BE AWESOME!

JUNE 1, 2023	JUNE 2, 2023	JUNE 3, 2023	JUNE 4, 2023
THURSDAY	FRIDAY	SATURDAY ○	SUNDAY
INTENTION:	INTENTION:	INTENTION:	INTENTION:

:	:	:	:
:	:	:	:
:	:	:	:
:	:	:	:
:	:	:	:
:	:	:	:
:	:	:	:
:	:	:	:
:	:	:	:
:	:	:	:
:	:	:	:
:	:	:	:
:	:	:	:
:	:	:	:
	:	:	:

HOW AM I SPENDING MY ENERGY?	HOW DO I AFFECT MY WORLD?	WHAT COULD I LET GO OF?	WHAT IS WORKING WELL FOR ME?
:	:	:	:
:	:	:	:
:	:	:	:
:	:	:	:
:	:	:	:
:	:	:	:
:	:	:	:
:	:	:	:
:	:	:	:
:	:	:	:
:	:	:	:

I AM GRATEFUL FOR:	I AM GRATEFUL FOR:	I AM GRATEFUL FOR:	I AM GRATEFUL FOR:

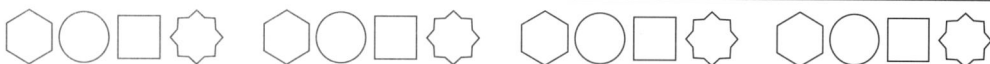

Top 3 Goals

_____

_____

_____

Weekly Alignment

Focus

Rituals For Thrivin

- EXERCISE
- MEDITATE / BREATHE
- JOURNAL
- DANCE
- GO ON A DATE
- CONNECT WITH NATURE
- VISUALIZE
- FAMILY TIME
- COOK / EAT A HEALTHY MEAL
- ORGANIZE MY SPACE / LIFE
- GET RID OF THINGS I DON'T LC
- BE WITH FRIENDS
- PLAY
- LET GO / FORGIVE
- SING / MAKE MUSIC
- CREATE ART
- READ FOR ENJOYMENT
- CONNECT / PRAY
- CALL SOMEONE / WRITE A LET
- STRETCH / DO YOGA
- MASSAGE / EXCHANGE TOUCH
- SERVE MY COMMUNITY
- TECHNOLOGY BREAK

Habit Tracking

⬡ = _____

◯ = _____

▢ = _____

✧ = _____

RITUALS FOR LIVING CHALLENGE

{ THIS WEEK, SIT IN FRONT OF A FIRE AT LEAST ONCE. IF YOU CAN'T GET TO A FIRE, SIT IN FRONT OF AS MANY CANDLES AS YOU CAN FIND. IMAGINE IT ENTERING YOU AND BURNING UP ANY NEGATIVITY WHILE FILLING YOUR BODY AND MIND WITH LIGHT. }

Wins from last week (what I gained / how I grew)

_____

_____

_____

How will I reframe something I find difficult, painful, or stressful?

_____

_____

_____

How will I create more freedom in my life this week?

_____

_____

Capture Your Brilliance - Dream, Expand, Record, Reflect:

Tasks

- MONTHLY PLAN
- INCOMPLETE FROM LAST WEEK
- LIFE DUTIES
- ★ STAR THE MOST IMPORTANT TASKS

JUNE 5, 2023	JUNE 6, 2023	JUNE 7, 2023
MONDAY	TUESDAY	WEDNESDAY
INTENTION:	INTENTION:	INTENTION:
:	:	:
:	:	:
:	:	:
:	:	:
:	:	:
:	:	:
:	:	:
:	:	:
:	:	:
:	:	:
:	:	:
:	:	:
:	:	:
:	:	:
WHAT SHALL I BE FOCUSED ON?	WHERE IS MY ATTENTION GOING?	WHAT PERSPECTIVE DO I CHOOSE?
:	:	:
:	:	:
:	:	:
:	:	:
:	:	:
:	:	:
:	:	:
:	:	:
:	:	:
:	:	:
:	:	:
:	:	:
I AM GRATEFUL FOR:	I AM GRATEFUL FOR:	I AM GRATEFUL FOR:

Final task: schedule next week!
NOW, PUT THESE TASKS & RITUALS
IN YOUR CALENDAR.
GO FORTH AND BE AWESOME!

JUNE 8, 2023	JUNE 9, 2023	JUNE 10, 2023	JUNE 11, 2023
THURSDAY	FRIDAY	SATURDAY ◑	SUNDAY
INTENTION:	INTENTION:	INTENTION:	INTENTION:
:	:	:	:
:	:	:	:
:	:	:	:
:	:	:	:
:	:	:	:
:	:	:	:
:	:	:	:
:	:	:	:
:	:	:	:
:	:	:	:
:	:	:	:
:	:	:	:
:	:	:	:
:	:	:	:
:	:	:	:
HOW AM I SPENDING MY ENERGY?	HOW DO I AFFECT MY WORLD?	WHAT COULD I LET GO OF?	WHAT IS WORKING WELL FOR ME?
:	:	:	:
:	:	:	:
:	:	:	:
:	:	:	:
:	:	:	:
:	:	:	:
:	:	:	:
:	:	:	:
:	:	:	:
:	:	:	:
:	:	:	:
:	:	:	:
I AM GRATEFUL FOR:	I AM GRATEFUL FOR:	I AM GRATEFUL FOR:	I AM GRATEFUL FOR:

169

JUNE 12 - JUNE 18, 2023

Top 3 Goals

_____

_____

_____

Weekly Alignment

Focus

Rituals For Thrivin

- EXERCISE
- MEDITATE / BREATHE
- JOURNAL
- DANCE
- GO ON A DATE
- CONNECT WITH NATURE
- VISUALIZE
- FAMILY TIME
- COOK / EAT A HEALTHY MEAL
- ORGANIZE MY SPACE / LIFE
- GET RID OF THINGS I DON'T LO
- BE WITH FRIENDS
- PLAY
- LET GO / FORGIVE
- SING / MAKE MUSIC
- CREATE ART
- READ FOR ENJOYMENT
- CONNECT / PRAY
- CALL SOMEONE / WRITE A LET
- STRETCH / DO YOGA
- MASSAGE / EXCHANGE TOUCH
- SERVE MY COMMUNITY
- TECHNOLOGY BREAK

Habit Tracking

⬡ = _____

◯ = _____

◻ = _____

✷ = _____

RITUALS FOR LIVING CHALLENGE

THIS WEEK, GET INTO A NATURAL BODY OF WATER. (OR AT LEAST TAKE 2 LONG BATHS.) AS YOU GET IN SET AN INTENTION, SUCH AS: TO BE DE-STRESSED, TO GO WITH THE FLOW, TO HAVE YOUR ENERGY NEUTRALIZED, TO BE CLEANSED, OR TO BE PUT BACK IN SYNC WITH NATURE.

Wins from last week (what I gained / how I grew)

_____
_____

How will I reframe something I find difficult, painful, or stressful?

_____
_____

How will I create more freedom in my life this week?

_____
_____

Capture Your Brilliance - Dream, Expand, Record, Reflect:

Connect to who you truly are beyond what the world tells you.

- The Well Life Book

Tasks

- MONTHLY PLAN
- INCOMPLETE FROM LAST WEEK
- LIFE DUTIES
- ★ STAR THE MOST IMPORTANT TASKS

JUNE 12, 2023	JUNE 13, 2023	JUNE 14, 2023
MONDAY	TUESDAY	WEDNESDAY
INTENTION:	INTENTION:	INTENTION:
:	:	:
:	:	:
:	:	:
:	:	:
:	:	:
:	:	:
:	:	:
:	:	:
:	:	:
:	:	:
:	:	:
:	:	:
:	:	:
:	:	:
:	:	:
WHAT SHALL I BE FOCUSED ON?	WHERE IS MY ATTENTION GOING?	WHAT PERSPECTIVE DO I CHOOSE?
:	:	:
:	:	:
:	:	:
:	:	:
:	:	:
:	:	:
:	:	:
:	:	:
:	:	:
:	:	:
:	:	:
I AM GRATEFUL FOR:	I AM GRATEFUL FOR:	I AM GRATEFUL FOR:

Final task: schedule next week!
NOW, PUT THESE TASKS & RITUALS
IN YOUR CALENDAR.
GO FORTH AND BE AWESOME!

JUNE 15, 2023	JUNE 16, 2023	JUNE 17, 2023	JUNE 18, 2023
THURSDAY	FRIDAY	SATURDAY	SUNDAY
INTENTION:	INTENTION:	INTENTION:	INTENTION:
:	:	:	:
:	:	:	:
:	:	:	:
:	:	:	:
:	:	:	:
:	:	:	:
:	:	:	:
:	:	:	:
:	:	:	:
:	:	:	:
:	:	:	:
:	:	:	:
:	:	:	:
:	:	:	:
:	:	:	:
HOW AM I SPENDING MY ENERGY?	HOW DO I AFFECT MY WORLD?	WHAT COULD I LET GO OF?	WHAT IS WORKING WELL FOR ME?
:	:	:	:
:	:	:	:
:	:	:	:
:	:	:	:
:	:	:	:
:	:	:	:
:	:	:	:
:	:	:	:
:	:	:	:
:	:	:	:
:	:	:	:
I AM GRATEFUL FOR:	I AM GRATEFUL FOR:	I AM GRATEFUL FOR:	I AM GRATEFUL FOR:

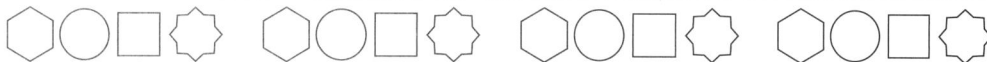

Top 3 Goals

_____

_____

_____

Weekly Alignment

Focus

Habit Tracking

⬡ = _____

◯ = _____

▢ = _____

⬗ = _____

Rituals For Thriving

- EXERCISE
- MEDITATE / BREATHE
- JOURNAL
- DANCE
- GO ON A DATE
- CONNECT WITH NATURE
- VISUALIZE
- FAMILY TIME
- COOK / EAT A HEALTHY MEAL
- ORGANIZE MY SPACE / LIFE
- GET RID OF THINGS I DON'T LOVE
- BE WITH FRIENDS
- PLAY
- LET GO / FORGIVE
- SING / MAKE MUSIC
- CREATE ART
- READ FOR ENJOYMENT
- CONNECT / PRAY
- CALL SOMEONE / WRITE A LETTER
- STRETCH / DO YOGA
- MASSAGE / EXCHANGE TOUCH
- SERVE MY COMMUNITY
- TECHNOLOGY BREAK

RITUALS FOR LIVING CHALLENGE

{ THIS WEEK, AT LEAST THREE TIMES, LIE ON YOUR BACK OUTDOORS, AND LOOK UP AT THE SKY. FEEL THE VASTNESS THAT YOU'RE PART OF. }

Wins from last week (what I gained / how I grew)

_____

_____

How will I reframe something I find difficult, painful, or stressful?

_____

_____

How will I create more freedom in my life this week?

_____

_____

Capture Your Brilliance - Dream, Expand, Record, Reflect:

Tasks

- MONTHLY PLAN
- INCOMPLETE FROM LAST WEEK
- LIFE DUTIES
- ★ STAR THE MOST IMPORTANT TASKS

JUNE 19, 2023	JUNE 20, 2023	JUNE 21, 2023
MONDAY	TUESDAY	WEDNESDAY
INTENTION:	INTENTION:	INTENTION:
:	:	:
:	:	:
:	:	:
:	:	:
:	:	:
:	:	:
:	:	:
:	:	:
:	:	:
:	:	:
:	:	:
:	:	:
:	:	:
:	:	:
:	:	:
WHAT SHALL I BE FOCUSED ON?	WHERE IS MY ATTENTION GOING?	WHAT PERSPECTIVE DO I CHOOSE?
:	:	:
:	:	:
:	:	:
:	:	:
:	:	:
:	:	:
:	:	:
:	:	:
:	:	:
:	:	:
:	:	:
:	:	:
I AM GRATEFUL FOR:	I AM GRATEFUL FOR:	I AM GRATEFUL FOR:

Final task: schedule next week!
NOW, PUT THESE TASKS & RITUALS
IN YOUR CALENDAR.
GO FORTH AND BE AWESOME!

JUNE 22, 2023	JUNE 23, 2023	JUNE 24, 2023	JUNE 25, 2023
THURSDAY	FRIDAY	SATURDAY	SUNDAY
INTENTION:	INTENTION:	INTENTION:	INTENTION:
:	:	:	:
:	:	:	:
:	:	:	:
:	:	:	:
:	:	:	:
:	:	:	:
:	:	:	:
:	:	:	:
:	:	:	:
:	:	:	:
:	:	:	:
:	:	:	:
:	:	:	:
:	:	:	:
:	:	:	:
:	:	:	:
HOW AM I SPENDING MY ENERGY?	HOW DO I AFFECT MY WORLD?	WHAT COULD I LET GO OF?	WHAT IS WORKING WELL FOR ME?
:	:	:	:
:	:	:	:
:	:	:	:
:	:	:	:
:	:	:	:
:	:	:	:
:	:	:	:
:	:	:	:
:	:	:	:
:	:	:	:
:	:	:	:
:	:	:	:
:	:	:	:
I AM GRATEFUL FOR:	I AM GRATEFUL FOR:	I AM GRATEFUL FOR:	I AM GRATEFUL FOR:

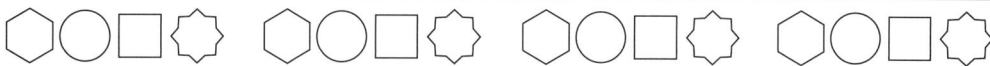

Life Edits

It's time to reflect on the past quarter, and decide what you want to refine as you move forward.

1. What was your biggest time and/or energy waster in the past quarter?

_____

2. Which activities and rituals yielded the biggest "return" for you (tangible or intangible) in the past quarter?

_____

_____

3. Review the habits you've been tracking in the last quarter. Reflect on the progress you've made and the habits you want to continue to work on as you move forward.

_____

_____

4. Is there anything you've been procrastinating over the past quarter?

_____

_____

5. What has been infringing on your happiness, health, or productivity in the past quarter that you intend to let go of in the coming quarter?

_____

_____

6. Self-Trust Personal Assessment: Compare your self-trust to the start of the year and see how you're doing. Rate your ability to trust yourself in each of the following areas of life on a scale of 0 to 10.

(Total lack of trust ⓪ ········ ⑩ Complete trust)

COMMUNICATION: How much do you trust yourself to tell the truth, say what needs to be said for healthy relationships, speak kindly, & express yourself authentically? _____

DEPENDABILITY: How much do you trust yourself to show up for friends and family, and support them when they need it? _____

TIME MANAGEMENT: How much do you trust yourself to be on time, to stick to your schedule and to plan appropriately? _____

FOLLOW THROUGH: How much do you trust yourself to follow through on your projects, in the time frame intended, to completion? _____

FOCUS: How much do you trust yourself to stay focused on what you have chosen to work on & avoid indulging in distraction? _____

MONEY: How much do you trust yourself to stay conscious of what you have, to maintain a positive attitude around money & to avoid taking on unnecessary debt? _____

HEALTH MAINTENANCE: How much do you trust yourself to treat your body & soul well, to get the care you need & to be kind to yourself? _____

NUTRITION: How much do you trust yourself to make good food choices, to eat in a healthy manner & to stick with your agreements around eating? _____

WORK PERFORMANCE: How much do you trust yourself to honor the work you do, to do your best & to show up enthusiastically? _____

VALUES: How much do you trust yourself to live by your core values? _____

Quarter Three Breakdown

1. Get into your *ritual for planning* space. Do whatever you do to tune in (light a candle, take a breath, go to a peaceful spot, set an intention, etc.).

2. Look back at your What I Will Accomplish This Year list, and find all the projects that will be occurring in the coming quarter. Write each one in the table below and mark the appropriate month number(s) for the month(s) in which it will taking place.

Project	Month		
	Jul	Aug	Sep
	①	②	③
	①	②	③
	①	②	③
	①	②	③
	①	②	③
	①	②	③
	①	②	③
	①	②	③
	①	②	③
	①	②	③
	①	②	③
	①	②	③
	①	②	③
	①	②	③
	①	②	③
	①	②	③
	①	②	③
	①	②	③
	①	②	③
	①	②	③
	①	②	③
	①	②	③
	①	②	③

July
Project Breakdown

1. Get into your *ritual for planning* space.

2. Gather the projects from the Quarterly Breakdown that pertain to this month and write each one on a PROJECT line below.

3. Under the project name, enter all of the tasks that are involved in the project. Each of these tasks must be a single action step so that it can be put into your calendar and when you see it, no analysis needs to occur – you know exactly what to do.

_____
PROJECT

_____   _____

_____   _____

_____   _____

_____   _____

_____   _____

_____   _____

_____   _____

_____
PROJECT

_____   _____

_____   _____

_____   _____

_____   _____

_____   _____

_____   _____

_____   _____

PROJECT

_____   _____
_____   _____
_____   _____
_____   _____
_____   _____
_____   _____
_____   _____

PROJECT

_____   _____
_____   _____
_____   _____
_____   _____
_____   _____
_____   _____
_____   _____

PROJECT

_____   _____
_____   _____
_____   _____
_____   _____
_____   _____
_____   _____
_____   _____

August
Project Breakdown

1. Get into your *ritual for planning* space.

2. Gather the projects from the Quarterly Breakdown that pertain to this month and write each one on a PROJECT line below.

3. Under the project name, enter all of the tasks that are involved in the project. Each of these tasks must be a single action step so that it can be put into your calendar and when you see it, no analysis needs to occur – you know exactly what to do.

PROJECT

PROJECT

PROJECT

_____   _____

_____   _____

_____   _____

_____   _____

_____   _____

_____   _____

_____   _____

PROJECT

_____   _____

_____   _____

_____   _____

_____   _____

_____   _____

_____   _____

_____   _____

PROJECT

_____   _____

_____   _____

_____   _____

_____   _____

_____   _____

_____   _____

_____   _____

September
Project Breakdown

1. Get into your *ritual for planning* space.

2. Gather the projects from the Quarterly Breakdown that pertain to this month and write each one on a PROJECT line below.

3. Under the project name, enter all of the tasks that are involved in the project. Each of these tasks must be a single action step so that it can be put into your calendar and when you see it, no analysis needs to occur – you know exactly what to do.

_____
PROJECT

_____   _____

_____   _____

_____   _____

_____   _____

_____   _____

_____   _____

_____   _____

_____
PROJECT

_____   _____

_____   _____

_____   _____

_____   _____

_____   _____

_____   _____

_____   _____

PROJECT

_____   _____
_____   _____
_____   _____
_____   _____
_____   _____
_____   _____
_____   _____

PROJECT

_____   _____
_____   _____
_____   _____
_____   _____
_____   _____
_____   _____
_____   _____

PROJECT

_____   _____
_____   _____
_____   _____
_____   _____
_____   _____
_____   _____

JULY

Monday	Tuesday	Wednesday
(26)	(27)	(28)
3 ○	4 U.S. Independence Day	5
10	11	12
17	18 Muharram Begins	19
24 ● / 31	25 ◐	26 Tisha B'Av Begins

Notes:

Thursday	Friday	Saturday	Sunday
(29)	(30)	1 Canada Day	2
6	7	8	9 ◑
13	14 Bastille Day (FR)	15	16
20	21	22	23 ♌ Leo
27	28	29	31

●: New Moon ◐: First Quarter ○: Full Moon ◑: Third Quarter

ates for moon phases are based on the Eastern Time Zone of the United States. In other parts of the world these phases may technically ur on the previous or following day. If precision is a concern, we encourage you to consult a moon phase calendar specific to your time zone.

Top 3 Goals

_____

_____

_____

Weekly Alignment

Focus

Rituals For Thriving

- ○ EXERCISE
- ○ MEDITATE / BREATHE
- ○ JOURNAL
- ○ DANCE
- ○ GO ON A DATE
- ○ CONNECT WITH NATURE
- ○ VISUALIZE
- ○ FAMILY TIME
- ○ COOK / EAT A HEALTHY MEAL
- ○ ORGANIZE MY SPACE / LIFE
- ○ GET RID OF THINGS I DON'T LO
- ○ BE WITH FRIENDS
- ○ PLAY
- ○ LET GO / FORGIVE
- ○ SING / MAKE MUSIC
- ○ CREATE ART
- ○ READ FOR ENJOYMENT
- ○ CONNECT / PRAY
- ○ CALL SOMEONE / WRITE A LE
- ○ STRETCH / DO YOGA
- ○ MASSAGE / EXCHANGE TOUCH
- ○ SERVE MY COMMUNITY
- ○ TECHNOLOGY BREAK

Habit Tracking

⬡ = _____

◯ = _____

▢ = _____

✧ = _____

RITUALS FOR LIVING CHALLENGE

{ THIS WEEK, PLANT A SEED, START A CUTTING, OR BUY A NEW PLANT. MAKE A COMMITMENT TO TAKE GOOD CARE OF IT. PLANTS CLEAN THE AIR, ADD BEAUTY TO OUR SURROUNDINGS, AND BRING LIFE TO OUR LIVING SPACE. }

Wins from last week (what I gained / how I grew)

_____

_____

How will I reframe something I find difficult, painful, or stressful?

_____

_____

How will I create more freedom in my life this week?

_____

_____

Capture Your Brilliance - Dream, Expand, Record, Reflect:

You add your own specialness and value to every circumstance.

- The Well Life Book

Tasks

- MONTHLY PLAN
- INCOMPLETE FROM LAST WEEK
- LIFE DUTIES
- ★ STAR THE MOST IMPORTANT TASKS

JUNE 26, 2023	JUNE 27, 2023	JUNE 28, 2023
MONDAY ☽	TUESDAY	WEDNESDAY
INTENTION:	INTENTION:	INTENTION:
:	:	:
:	:	:
:	:	:
:	:	:
:	:	:
:	:	:
:	:	:
:	:	:
:	:	:
:	:	:
:	:	:
:	:	:
:	:	:
:	:	:
:	:	:
WHAT SHALL I BE FOCUSED ON?	WHERE IS MY ATTENTION GOING?	WHAT PERSPECTIVE DO I CHOOSE
:	:	:
:	:	:
:	:	:
:	:	:
:	:	:
:	:	:
:	:	:
:	:	:
:	:	:
:	:	:
:	:	:
:	:	:
:	:	:
	:	
I AM GRATEFUL FOR:	I AM GRATEFUL FOR:	I AM GRATEFUL FOR:

Final task: schedule next week!
NOW, PUT THESE TASKS & RITUALS
IN YOUR CALENDAR.
GO FORTH AND BE AWESOME!

JULY 29, 2023	JUNE 30, 2023	JULY 1, 2023	JULY 2, 2023
THURSDAY	FRIDAY	SATURDAY	SUNDAY
INTENTION:	INTENTION:	INTENTION:	INTENTION:
:	:	:	:
:	:	:	:
:	:	:	:
:	:	:	:
:	:	:	:
:	:	:	:
:	:	:	:
:	:	:	:
:	:	:	:
:	:	:	:
:	:	:	:
:	:	:	:
:	:	:	:
:	:	:	:
:	:	:	:
:	:	:	:
HOW AM I SPENDING MY ENERGY?	HOW DO I AFFECT MY WORLD?	WHAT COULD I LET GO OF?	WHAT IS WORKING WELL FOR ME?
:	:	:	:
:	:	:	:
:	:	:	:
:	:	:	:
:	:	:	:
:	:	:	:
:	:	:	:
:	:	:	:
:	:	:	:
:	:	:	:
:	:	:	:
I AM GRATEFUL FOR:	I AM GRATEFUL FOR:	I AM GRATEFUL FOR:	I AM GRATEFUL FOR:

Top 3 Goals

_____

_____

_____

Weekly Alignment

Focus

Rituals For Thrivin

- o EXERCISE
- o MEDITATE / BREATHE
- o JOURNAL
- o DANCE
- o GO ON A DATE
- o CONNECT WITH NATURE
- o VISUALIZE
- o FAMILY TIME
- o COOK / EAT A HEALTHY MEAL
- o ORGANIZE MY SPACE / LIFE
- o GET RID OF THINGS I DON'T L(
- o BE WITH FRIENDS
- o PLAY
- o LET GO / FORGIVE
- o SING / MAKE MUSIC
- o CREATE ART
- o READ FOR ENJOYMENT
- o CONNECT / PRAY
- o CALL SOMEONE / WRITE A LE
- o STRETCH / DO YOGA
- o MASSAGE / EXCHANGE TOUC
- o SERVE MY COMMUNITY
- o TECHNOLOGY BREAK

Habit Tracking

⬡ = _____

◯ = _____

☐ = _____

⬡ = _____

RITUALS FOR LIVING CHALLENGE

{ THIS WEEK, CONSUME AS LITTLE SWEETENER AS POSSIBLE, INCLUDING WHITE SUGAR, CORN SYRUP, AGAVE NECTAR, HONEY, MAPLE SYRUP, FRUIT JUICE, RICE SYRUP, EVAPORATED CANE JUICE, ETC. HUMANS EAT MORE SWEETENER THAN EVER BEFORE. BREAK YOUR ADDICTION. }

Wins from last week (what I gained / how I grew)

_____

_____

How will I reframe something I find difficult, painful, or stressful?

_____

_____

How will I create more freedom in my life this week?

_____

_____

Capture Your Brilliance - Dream, Expand, Record, Reflect:

Find your gifts, own your gifts, bring your gifts to the forefront of your life.

- The Well Life Book

Tasks

- MONTHLY PLAN
- INCOMPLETE FROM LAST WEEK
- LIFE DUTIES
- ★ STAR THE MOST IMPORTANT TASKS

JULY 3, 2023	JULY 4, 2023	JULY 5, 2023
MONDAY ○	TUESDAY	WEDNESDAY
INTENTION:	INTENTION:	INTENTION:
:	:	:
:	:	:
:	:	:
:	:	:
:	:	:
:	:	:
:	:	:
:	:	:
:	:	:
:	:	:
:	:	:
:	:	:
:	:	:
:	:	:
:	:	:
WHAT SHALL I BE FOCUSED ON?	WHERE IS MY ATTENTION GOING?	WHAT PERSPECTIVE DO I CHOOSE?
:	:	:
:	:	:
:	:	:
:	:	:
:	:	:
:	:	:
:	:	:
:	:	:
:	:	:
:	:	:
:	:	:
:	:	:
I AM GRATEFUL FOR:	I AM GRATEFUL FOR:	I AM GRATEFUL FOR:

Final task: schedule next week!
NOW, PUT THESE TASKS & RITUALS
IN YOUR CALENDAR.
GO FORTH AND BE AWESOME!

JULY 6, 2023	JULY 7, 2023	JULY 8, 2023	JULY 9, 2023
THURSDAY	FRIDAY	SATURDAY	SUNDAY ◑
INTENTION:	INTENTION:	INTENTION:	INTENTION:
:	:	:	:
:	:	:	:
:	:	:	:
:	:	:	:
:	:	:	:
:	:	:	:
:	:	:	:
:	:	:	:
:	:	:	:
:	:	:	:
:	:	:	:
:	:	:	:
:	:	:	:
:	:	:	:
:	:	:	:
HOW AM I SPENDING MY ENERGY?	HOW DO I AFFECT MY WORLD?	WHAT COULD I LET GO OF?	WHAT IS WORKING WELL FOR ME?
:	:	:	:
:	:	:	:
:	:	:	:
:	:	:	:
:	:	:	:
:	:	:	:
:	:	:	:
:	:	:	:
:	:	:	:
:	:	:	:
:	:	:	:
:	:	:	:
I AM GRATEFUL FOR:	I AM GRATEFUL FOR:	I AM GRATEFUL FOR:	I AM GRATEFUL FOR:

Top 3 Goals

_____

_____

_____

Weekly Alignment

Focus

Rituals For Thriving

- o EXERCISE
- o MEDITATE / BREATHE
- o JOURNAL
- o DANCE
- o GO ON A DATE
- o CONNECT WITH NATURE
- o VISUALIZE
- o FAMILY TIME
- o COOK / EAT A HEALTHY MEAL
- o ORGANIZE MY SPACE / LIFE
- o GET RID OF THINGS I DON'T LO'
- o BE WITH FRIENDS
- o PLAY
- o LET GO / FORGIVE
- o SING / MAKE MUSIC
- o CREATE ART
- o READ FOR ENJOYMENT
- o CONNECT / PRAY
- o CALL SOMEONE / WRITE A LET
- o STRETCH / DO YOGA
- o MASSAGE / EXCHANGE TOUCH
- o SERVE MY COMMUNITY
- o TECHNOLOGY BREAK

Habit Tracking

◯ = _____

◯ = _____

▢ = _____

✿ = _____

RITUALS FOR LIVING CHALLENGE

{ THIS WEEK IS A SELF-LOVE FEST. APOLOGIZE FOR THE WAYS YOU'VE MISTREATED, CRITICIZED, NEGLECTED, & WITHHELD LOVE FROM YOUR-SELF. TELL YOURSELF, "I LOVE YOU, [NAME]." BE SWEET TO YOURSELF. TAKE YOURSELF ON A DATE. CHERISH YOURSELF, HONOR YOURSELF. }

Wins from last week (what I gained / how I grew)

_____

_____

_____

How will I reframe something I find difficult, painful, or stressful?

_____

_____

_____

How will I create more freedom in my life this week?

_____

_____

Capture Your Brilliance - Dream, Expand, Record, Reflect:

Tasks

- MONTHLY PLAN
- INCOMPLETE FROM LAST WEEK
- LIFE DUTIES
- ★ STAR THE MOST IMPORTANT TASKS

JULY 10, 2023	JULY 11, 2023	JULY 12, 2023
MONDAY	TUESDAY	WEDNESDAY ○
INTENTION:	INTENTION:	INTENTION:
:	:	:
:	:	:
:	:	:
:	:	:
:	:	:
:	:	:
:	:	:
:	:	:
:	:	:
:	:	:
:	:	:
:	:	:
:	:	:
:	:	:
WHAT SHALL I BE FOCUSED ON?	WHERE IS MY ATTENTION GOING?	WHAT PERSPECTIVE DO I CHOOSE?
:	:	:
:	:	:
:	:	:
:	:	:
:	:	:
:	:	:
:	:	:
:	:	:
:	:	:
:	:	:
:	:	:
:	:	:
:	:	
I AM GRATEFUL FOR:	I AM GRATEFUL FOR:	I AM GRATEFUL FOR:

Final task: schedule next week!
NOW, PUT THESE TASKS & RITUALS
IN YOUR CALENDAR,
GO FORTH AND BE AWESOME!

JULY 13, 2023	JULY 14, 2023	JULY 15, 2023	JULY 16, 2023
THURSDAY	FRIDAY	SATURDAY	SUNDAY
INTENTION:	INTENTION:	INTENTION:	INTENTION:
:	:	:	:
:	:	:	:
:	:	:	:
:	:	:	:
:	:	:	:
:	:	:	:
:	:	:	:
:	:	:	:
:	:	:	:
:	:	:	:
:	:	:	:
:	:	:	:
:	:	:	:
:	:	:	:
:	:	:	:
:	:	:	:
HOW AM I SPENDING MY ENERGY?	HOW DO I AFFECT MY WORLD?	WHAT COULD I LET GO OF?	WHAT IS WORKING WELL FOR ME?
:	:	:	:
:	:	:	:
.	:	.	:
:	:	:	:
:	:	:	:
:	:	:	:
:	:	:	:
:	:	:	:
:	:	:	:
:	:	:	:
:	:	:	:
:	:	:	:
I AM GRATEFUL FOR:	I AM GRATEFUL FOR:	I AM GRATEFUL FOR:	I AM GRATEFUL FOR:

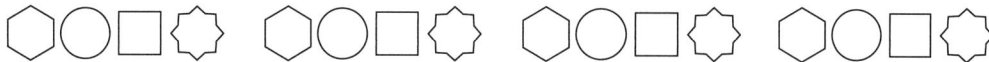

Top 3 Goals

_____

_____

_____

Weekly Alignment

Focus

Habit Tracking

⬡ = _____

◯ = _____

▢ = _____

✦ = _____

Rituals For Thriving

- o EXERCISE
- o MEDITATE / BREATHE
- o JOURNAL
- o DANCE
- o GO ON A DATE
- o CONNECT WITH NATURE
- o VISUALIZE
- o FAMILY TIME
- o COOK / EAT A HEALTHY MEAL
- o ORGANIZE MY SPACE / LIFE
- o GET RID OF THINGS I DON'T LO
- o BE WITH FRIENDS
- o PLAY
- o LET GO / FORGIVE
- o SING / MAKE MUSIC
- o CREATE ART
- o READ FOR ENJOYMENT
- o CONNECT / PRAY
- o CALL SOMEONE / WRITE A LET
- o STRETCH / DO YOGA
- o MASSAGE / EXCHANGE TOUCH
- o SERVE MY COMMUNITY
- o TECHNOLOGY BREAK

RITUALS FOR LIVING CHALLENGE

{ THIS WEEK, AT LEAST TWICE, INVITE SOMEONE TO SHARE A MEAL WITH YOU. EXTRA CREDIT: COOK THE MEAL YOURSELF. }

Wins from last week (what I gained / how I grew)

_____

_____

_____

How will I reframe something I find difficult, painful, or stressful?

_____

_____

_____

How will I create more freedom in my life this week?

_____

_____

Capture Your Brilliance - Dream, Expand, Record, Reflect:

There's no good reason to deprive the world of your greatness.
- The Well Life Book

Tasks

- MONTHLY PLAN
- INCOMPLETE FROM LAST WEEK
- LIFE DUTIES
- ★ STAR THE MOST IMPORTANT TASKS

JULY 17, 2023	JULY 18, 2023	JULY 19, 2023
MONDAY ●	TUESDAY	WEDNESDAY
INTENTION:	INTENTION:	INTENTION:
:	:	:
:	:	:
:	:	:
:	:	:
:	:	:
:	:	:
:	:	:
:	:	:
:	:	:
:	:	:
:	:	:
:	:	:
:	:	:
WHAT SHALL I BE FOCUSED ON?	WHERE IS MY ATTENTION GOING?	WHAT PERSPECTIVE DO I CHOOSE?
:	:	:
:	:	:
:	:	:
:	:	:
:	:	:
:	:	:
:	:	:
:	:	:
:	:	:
:	:	:
:	:	:
:	:	:
I AM GRATEFUL FOR:	I AM GRATEFUL FOR:	I AM GRATEFUL FOR:

Final task: schedule next week!
NOW, PUT THESE TASKS & RITUALS
IN YOUR CALENDAR.
GO FORTH AND BE AWESOME!

JULY 20, 2023	JULY 21, 2023	JULY 22, 2023	JULY 23, 2023
THURSDAY	FRIDAY	SATURDAY	SUNDAY
INTENTION:	INTENTION:	INTENTION:	INTENTION:
:	:	:	:
:	:	:	:
:	:	:	:
:	:	:	:
:	:	:	:
:	:	:	:
:	:	:	:
:	:	:	:
:	:	:	:
:	:	:	:
:	:	:	:
:	:	:	:
:	:	:	:
:	:	:	:
:	:	:	:
HOW AM I SPENDING MY ENERGY?	HOW DO I AFFECT MY WORLD?	WHAT COULD I LET GO OF?	WHAT IS WORKING WELL FOR ME?
:	:	:	:
:	:	:	:
:	:	:	:
:	:	:	:
:	:	:	:
:	:	:	:
:	:	:	:
:	:	:	:
:	:	:	:
:	:	:	:
:	:	:	:
:	:	:	:
I AM GRATEFUL FOR:	I AM GRATEFUL FOR:	I AM GRATEFUL FOR:	I AM GRATEFUL FOR:

Top 3 Goals

_____

_____

_____

Weekly Alignment

Focus

Habit Tracking

⬡ = _____

◯ = _____

☐ = _____

✦ = _____

RITUALS FOR LIVING CHALLENGE

{ THIS WEEK, AT LEAST ONCE, GIVE YOURSELF A FOOT MASSAGE FOR AT LEAST TEN MINUTES PER FOOT. USE SOME OIL OR LOTION. IF YOU DON'T HAVE FEET OR CAN'T REACH THEM, MASSAGE ANOTHER PART OF YOUR BODY – OR, FOR EXTRA CREDIT – YOUR WHOLE BODY. }

Rituals For Thriving

- EXERCISE
- MEDITATE / BREATHE
- JOURNAL
- DANCE
- GO ON A DATE
- CONNECT WITH NATURE
- VISUALIZE
- FAMILY TIME
- COOK / EAT A HEALTHY MEAL
- ORGANIZE MY SPACE / LIFE
- GET RID OF THINGS I DON'T LOVE
- BE WITH FRIENDS
- PLAY
- LET GO / FORGIVE
- SING / MAKE MUSIC
- CREATE ART
- READ FOR ENJOYMENT
- CONNECT / PRAY
- CALL SOMEONE / WRITE A LETTER
- STRETCH / DO YOGA
- MASSAGE / EXCHANGE TOUCH
- SERVE MY COMMUNITY
- TECHNOLOGY BREAK

Wins from last week (what I gained / how I grew)

_____

_____

How will I reframe something I find difficult, painful, or stressful?

_____

_____

How will I create more freedom in my life this week?

_____

_____

Capture Your Brilliance - Dream, Expand, Record, Reflect:

Tasks

- MONTHLY PLAN
- INCOMPLETE FROM LAST WEEK
- LIFE DUTIES
- ★ STAR THE MOST IMPORTANT TASKS

JULY 24, 2023	JULY 25, 2023	JULY 26, 2023
MONDAY	TUESDAY ◑	WEDNESDAY
INTENTION:	INTENTION:	INTENTION:
:	:	:
:	:	:
:	:	:
:	:	:
:	:	:
:	:	:
:	:	:
:	:	:
:	:	:
:	:	:
:	:	:
:	:	:
:	:	:
:	:	:
WHAT SHALL I BE FOCUSED ON?	WHERE IS MY ATTENTION GOING?	WHAT PERSPECTIVE DO I CHOOSE?
:	:	:
:	:	:
:	:	:
:	:	:
:	:	:
:	:	:
:	:	:
:	:	:
:	:	:
:	:	:
:	:	:
I AM GRATEFUL FOR:	I AM GRATEFUL FOR:	I AM GRATEFUL FOR:

Final task: schedule next week!
NOW, PUT THESE TASKS & RITUALS
IN YOUR CALENDAR.
GO FORTH AND BE AWESOME!

JULY 27, 2023	JULY 28, 2023	JULY 29, 2023	JULY 30, 2023
THURSDAY	FRIDAY	SATURDAY	SUNDAY
INTENTION:	INTENTION:	INTENTION:	INTENTION:
:	:	:	:
:	:	:	:
:	:	:	:
:	:	:	:
:	:	:	:
:	:	:	:
:	:	:	:
:	:	:	:
:	:	:	:
:	:	:	:
:	:	:	:
:	:	:	:
:	:	:	:
:	:	:	:
:	:	:	:
	:	:	:
HOW AM I SPENDING MY ENERGY?	HOW DO I AFFECT MY WORLD?	WHAT COULD I LET GO OF?	WHAT IS WORKING WELL FOR ME?
:	:	:	:
:	:	:	:
.	.	.	.
:	:	:	:
:	:	:	:
:	:	:	:
:	:	:	:
:	:	:	:
:	:	:	:
:	:	:	:
:	:	:	:
:	:	:	:
	:	:	:
I AM GRATEFUL FOR:	I AM GRATEFUL FOR:	I AM GRATEFUL FOR:	I AM GRATEFUL FOR:

AUGUST

Monday	Tuesday	Wednesday
(31)	1 ○	2
7	8 ◑	9
14	15	16 ●
21	22	23 ♍ Virgo
28	29	30 ○

Notes:

Thursday	Friday	Saturday	Sunday
3	4	5	6
10	11	12	13
17	18	19	20
24	25	26	27
31	(1)	(2)	(3)

In the 24 cell: ◑

●: New Moon ◐: First Quarter ○: Full Moon ◑: Third Quarter

ates for moon phases are based on the Eastern Time Zone of the United States. In other parts of the world these phases may technically ur on the previous or following day. If precision is a concern, we encourage you to consult a moon phase calendar specific to your time zone.

Top 3 Goals

_____

_____

_____

Weekly Alignment

Focus

Habit Tracking

⬡ = _____

◯ = _____

▢ = _____

⬗ = _____

Rituals For Thriving

- ○ EXERCISE
- ○ MEDITATE / BREATHE
- ○ JOURNAL
- ○ DANCE
- ○ GO ON A DATE
- ○ CONNECT WITH NATURE
- ○ VISUALIZE
- ○ FAMILY TIME
- ○ COOK / EAT A HEALTHY MEAL
- ○ ORGANIZE MY SPACE / LIFE
- ○ GET RID OF THINGS I DON'T LOV
- ○ BE WITH FRIENDS
- ○ PLAY
- ○ LET GO / FORGIVE
- ○ SING / MAKE MUSIC
- ○ CREATE ART
- ○ READ FOR ENJOYMENT
- ○ CONNECT / PRAY
- ○ CALL SOMEONE / WRITE A LET
- ○ STRETCH / DO YOGA
- ○ MASSAGE / EXCHANGE TOUCH
- ○ SERVE MY COMMUNITY
- ○ TECHNOLOGY BREAK

RITUALS FOR LIVING CHALLENGE

{ THIS WEEK, TRY NETI (NASAL IRRIGATION) 3 TIMES. ADD ¼ TO ½ TEASPOON SALT TO ONE CUP OF WARM, CLEAN WATER. USING A NETI POT, STAND OVER A SINK, TIP YOUR HEAD TO THE SIDE, AND POUR HALF THROUGH ONE NOSTRIL AND HALF THROUGH THE OTHER. FOLLOW BY PLACING A FEW DROPS OF OIL IN EACH NOSTRIL. }

Wins from last week (what I gained / how I grew)

_____

_____

_____

How will I reframe something I find difficult, painful, or stressful?

_____

_____

_____

How will I create more freedom in my life this week?

_____

_____

Capture Your Brilliance - Dream, Expand, Record, Reflect:

If you're guided by your purpose, life won't feel like a missed opportunity.

- The Well Life Book

Tasks

- MONTHLY PLAN
- INCOMPLETE FROM LAST WEEK
- LIFE DUTIES
- ★ STAR THE MOST IMPORTANT TASKS

| JULY 31, 2023 | AUGUST 1, 2023 | AUGUST 2, 2023 |
MONDAY	TUESDAY ◯	WEDNESDAY
INTENTION:	INTENTION:	INTENTION:
:	:	:
:	:	:
:	:	:
:	:	:
:	:	:
:	:	:
:	:	:
:	:	:
:	:	:
:	:	:
:	:	:
:	:	:
:	:	:
:	:	:
:	:	:
WHAT SHALL I BE FOCUSED ON?	WHERE IS MY ATTENTION GOING?	WHAT PERSPECTIVE DO I CHOOSE
:	:	:
:	:	:
:	:	:
:	:	:
:	:	:
:	:	:
:	:	:
:	:	:
:	:	:
:	:	:
:	:	:
:	:	:
I AM GRATEFUL FOR:	I AM GRATEFUL FOR:	I AM GRATEFUL FOR:

Final task: schedule next week!
NOW, PUT THESE TASKS & RITUALS
IN YOUR CALENDAR.
GO FORTH AND BE AWESOME!

AUGUST 3, 2023	AUGUST 4, 2023	AUGUST 5, 2023	AUGUST 6, 2023
THURSDAY	FRIDAY	SATURDAY	SUNDAY
INTENTION:	INTENTION:	INTENTION:	INTENTION:

HOW AM I SPENDING MY ENERGY?	HOW DO I AFFECT MY WORLD?	WHAT COULD I LET GO OF?	WHAT IS WORKING WELL FOR ME?

I AM GRATEFUL FOR:	I AM GRATEFUL FOR:	I AM GRATEFUL FOR:	I AM GRATEFUL FOR:

Top 3 Goals

_____

_____

_____

Weekly Alignment

Focus

Habit Tracking

⬡ = _____

◯ = _____

▢ = _____

✺ = _____

Rituals For Thriving

- ○ EXERCISE
- ○ MEDITATE / BREATHE
- ○ JOURNAL
- ○ DANCE
- ○ GO ON A DATE
- ○ CONNECT WITH NATURE
- ○ VISUALIZE
- ○ FAMILY TIME
- ○ COOK / EAT A HEALTHY MEAL
- ○ ORGANIZE MY SPACE / LIFE
- ○ GET RID OF THINGS I DON'T LOV
- ○ BE WITH FRIENDS
- ○ PLAY
- ○ LET GO / FORGIVE
- ○ SING / MAKE MUSIC
- ○ CREATE ART
- ○ READ FOR ENJOYMENT
- ○ CONNECT / PRAY
- ○ CALL SOMEONE / WRITE A LET
- ○ STRETCH / DO YOGA
- ○ MASSAGE / EXCHANGE TOUCH
- ○ SERVE MY COMMUNITY
- ○ TECHNOLOGY BREAK

RITUALS FOR LIVING CHALLENGE

{ THIS WEEK, FIND A WAY TO LAUGH EACH DAY. WATCH A COMEDY, HAVE SOMEONE TICKLE YOU, MAKE FACES IN THE MIRROR, DO SOMETHING RIDICULOUS, OR JUST START BELLY LAUGHING LOUDLY UNTIL IT TURNS INTO NATURAL LAUGHTER. }

Wins from last week (what I gained / how I grew)

_____

_____

_____

How will I reframe something I find difficult, painful, or stressful?

_____

_____

_____

How will I create more freedom in my life this week?

_____

_____

Capture Your Brilliance - Dream, Expand, Record, Reflect:

Tasks

- MONTHLY PLAN
- INCOMPLETE FROM LAST WEEK
- LIFE DUTIES
- ★ STAR THE MOST IMPORTANT TASKS

AUGUST 7, 2023	AUGUST 8, 2023	AUGUST 9, 2023
MONDAY	TUESDAY ◐	WEDNESDAY
INTENTION:	INTENTION:	INTENTION:
:	:	:
:	:	:
:	:	:
:	:	:
:	:	:
:	:	:
:	:	:
:	:	:
:	:	:
:	:	:
:	:	:
:	:	:
:	:	:
:	:	:
:	:	:
WHAT SHALL I BE FOCUSED ON?	WHERE IS MY ATTENTION GOING?	WHAT PERSPECTIVE DO I CHOOSE
:	:	:
:	:	:
:	:	:
:	:	:
:	:	:
:	:	:
:	:	:
:	:	:
:	:	:
:	:	:
:	:	:
:	:	:
I AM GRATEFUL FOR:	I AM GRATEFUL FOR:	I AM GRATEFUL FOR:

Final task: schedule next week!

NOW, PUT THESE TASKS & RITUALS
IN YOUR CALENDAR.
GO FORTH AND BE AWESOME!

216

AUGUST 10, 2023	AUGUST 11, 2023	AUGUST 12, 2023	AUGUST 13, 2023
THURSDAY	FRIDAY	SATURDAY	SUNDAY
INTENTION:	INTENTION:	INTENTION:	INTENTION:

HOW AM I SPENDING MY ENERGY?	HOW DO I AFFECT MY WORLD?	WHAT COULD I LET GO OF?	WHAT IS WORKING WELL FOR ME?

I AM GRATEFUL FOR:	I AM GRATEFUL FOR:	I AM GRATEFUL FOR:	I AM GRATEFUL FOR:

Top 3 Goals

_____

_____

_____

Weekly Alignment

Focus

Rituals For Thriving

- o EXERCISE
- o MEDITATE / BREATHE
- o JOURNAL
- o DANCE
- o GO ON A DATE
- o CONNECT WITH NATURE
- o VISUALIZE
- o FAMILY TIME
- o COOK / EAT A HEALTHY MEAL
- o ORGANIZE MY SPACE / LIFE
- o GET RID OF THINGS I DON'T LO
- o BE WITH FRIENDS
- o PLAY
- o LET GO / FORGIVE
- o SING / MAKE MUSIC
- o CREATE ART
- o READ FOR ENJOYMENT
- o CONNECT / PRAY
- o CALL SOMEONE / WRITE A LET
- o STRETCH / DO YOGA
- o MASSAGE / EXCHANGE TOUCH
- o SERVE MY COMMUNITY
- o TECHNOLOGY BREAK

Habit Tracking

◯ = _____

◯ = _____

☐ = _____

✧ = _____

RITUALS FOR LIVING CHALLENGE

{ THIS WEEK, GENERATE AS LITTLE GARBAGE AS POSSIBLE. RECYCLE EVERYTHING YOU CAN (TRY TO REDUCE YOUR RECYCLABLES TOO), COMPOST ANYTHING YOU CAN, AVOID SINGLE-USE AND SINGLE-SERVING PACKAGING, AND BUY LESS STUFF THAT WILL END UP IN A LANDFILL. }

Wins from last week (what I gained / how I grew)

_____

_____

_____

How will I reframe something I find difficult, painful, or stressful?

_____

_____

_____

How will I create more freedom in my life this week?

_____

_____

Capture Your Brilliance - Dream, Expand, Record, Reflect:

Receiving is half of the equation of creating something new or initiating a change.

- The Well Life Book

Tasks

- MONTHLY PLAN
- INCOMPLETE FROM LAST WEEK
- LIFE DUTIES
- ★ STAR THE MOST IMPORTANT TASKS

AUGUST 14, 2023	AUGUST 15, 2023	AUGUST 16, 2023
MONDAY	TUESDAY	WEDNESDAY
INTENTION:	INTENTION:	INTENTION:
:	:	:
:	:	:
:	:	:
:	:	:
:	:	:
:	:	:
:	:	:
:	:	:
:	:	:
:	:	:
:	:	:
:	:	:
:	:	:
:	:	:
WHAT SHALL I BE FOCUSED ON?	WHERE IS MY ATTENTION GOING?	WHAT PERSPECTIVE DO I CHOOS
:	:	:
:	:	:
:	:	:
:	:	:
:	:	:
:	:	:
:	:	:
:	:	:
:	:	:
:	:	:
I AM GRATEFUL FOR:	I AM GRATEFUL FOR:	I AM GRATEFUL FOR

Final task: schedule next week!
NOW, PUT THESE TASKS & RITUALS
IN YOUR CALENDAR,
GO FORTH AND BE AWESOME!

AUGUST 17, 2023	AUGUST 18, 2023	AUGUST 19, 2023	AUGUST 20, 2023
THURSDAY	FRIDAY	SATURDAY	SUNDAY
INTENTION:	INTENTION:	INTENTION:	INTENTION:
:	:	:	:
:	:	:	:
:	:	:	:
:	:	:	:
:	:	:	:
:	:	:	:
:	:	:	:
:	:	:	:
:	:	:	:
:	:	:	:
:	:	:	:
:	:	:	:
:	:	:	:
:	:	:	:
HOW AM I SPENDING MY ENERGY?	HOW DO I AFFECT MY WORLD?	WHAT COULD I LET GO OF?	WHAT IS WORKING WELL FOR ME?
:	:	:	:
:	:	:	:
:	:	:	:
:	:	:	:
:	:	:	:
:	:	:	:
:	:	:	:
:	:	:	:
:	:	:	:
:	:	:	:
:	:	:	:
:	:	:	:
I AM GRATEFUL FOR:	I AM GRATEFUL FOR:	I AM GRATEFUL FOR:	I AM GRATEFUL FOR:

Top 3 Goals

_____

_____

_____

Weekly Alignment

Focus

Rituals For Thriving

- o EXERCISE
- o MEDITATE / BREATHE
- o JOURNAL
- o DANCE
- o GO ON A DATE
- o CONNECT WITH NATURE
- o VISUALIZE
- o FAMILY TIME
- o COOK / EAT A HEALTHY MEAL
- o ORGANIZE MY SPACE / LIFE
- o GET RID OF THINGS I DON'T LO
- o BE WITH FRIENDS
- o PLAY
- o LET GO / FORGIVE
- o SING / MAKE MUSIC
- o CREATE ART
- o READ FOR ENJOYMENT
- o CONNECT / PRAY
- o CALL SOMEONE / WRITE A LE
- o STRETCH / DO YOGA
- o MASSAGE / EXCHANGE TOUCH
- o SERVE MY COMMUNITY
- o TECHNOLOGY BREAK

Habit Tracking

⬡ = _____

◯ = _____

☐ = _____

✧ = _____

RITUALS FOR LIVING CHALLENGE

{ OPTIMIZE BOWEL HEALTH THIS WEEK. HAVE PLENTY OF WATER, LOTS OF FIBER (VEGGIES, FRUITS, BEANS, OATS), GOOD FATS (OLIVE OIL, FLAX, AVOCADO, HEMP, CHIA, ETC.), EXERCISE YOUR ABDOMEN, EAT CULTURED FOODS, DE-STRESS, AND TRY SQUATTING WHEN YOU GO. }

Wins from last week (what I gained / how I grew)

_____

_____

How will I reframe something I find difficult, painful, or stressful?

_____

_____

How will I create more freedom in my life this week?

_____

_____

Capture Your Brilliance - Dream, Expand, Record, Reflect:

Tasks

- MONTHLY PLAN
- INCOMPLETE FROM LAST WEEK
- LIFE DUTIES
- ★ STAR THE MOST IMPORTANT TASKS

AUGUST 21, 2023	AUGUST 22, 2023	AUGUST 23, 2023
MONDAY	TUESDAY	WEDNESDAY
INTENTION:	INTENTION:	INTENTION:
:	:	:
:	:	:
:	:	:
:	:	:
:	:	:
:	:	:
:	:	:
:	:	:
:	:	:
:	:	:
:	:	:
:	:	:
:	:	:
:	:	:
:	:	:
	:	:
WHAT SHALL I BE FOCUSED ON?	WHERE IS MY ATTENTION GOING?	WHAT PERSPECTIVE DO I CHOOS
:	:	:
:	:	:
:	:	:
:	:	:
:	:	:
:	:	:
:	:	:
:	:	:
:	:	:
:	:	:
:	:	:
:	:	:
I AM GRATEFUL FOR:	I AM GRATEFUL FOR:	I AM GRATEFUL FOR

Final task: schedule next week!
NOW, PUT THESE TASKS & RITUALS
IN YOUR CALENDAR.
GO FORTH AND BE AWESOME!

AUGUST 24, 2023	AUGUST 25, 2023	AUGUST 26, 2023	AUGUST 27, 2023
THURSDAY	FRIDAY	SATURDAY	SUNDAY
INTENTION:	INTENTION:	INTENTION:	INTENTION:
:	:	:	:
:	:	:	:
:	:	:	:
:	:	:	:
:	:	:	:
:	:	:	:
:	:	:	:
:	:	:	:
:	:	:	:
:	:	:	:
:	:	:	:
:	:	:	:
:	:	:	:
:	:	:	:
:	:	:	:
HOW AM I SPENDING MY ENERGY?	HOW DO I AFFECT MY WORLD?	WHAT COULD I LET GO OF?	WHAT IS WORKING WELL FOR ME?
:	:	:	:
:	:	:	:
:	:	:	:
:	:	:	:
:	:	:	:
:	:	:	:
:	:	:	:
:	:	:	:
:	:	:	:
:	:	:	:
:	:	:	:
:	:	:	:
:	:	:	:
I AM GRATEFUL FOR:	I AM GRATEFUL FOR:	I AM GRATEFUL FOR:	I AM GRATEFUL FOR:

Monday	Tuesday	Wednesday
(28)	(29)	(30)
4 Labor Day	5 International Day of Charity	6 ◐
11	12	13
18	19	20
25	26	27

Notes:

SEPTEMBER

Thursday	Friday	Saturday	Sunday
(31)	1	2	3
7	8	9	10
14 ●	15 Rosh Hashana Begins	16	17
21	22 Autumn Equinox ◑	23 ♎ Libra	24 Yom Kippur Begins
28	29 ○	30	(1)

New Moon ●: First Quarter ○: Full Moon ◑: Third Quarter

tes for moon phases are based on the Eastern Time Zone of the United States. In other parts of the world these phases may technically
ur on the previous or following day. If precision is a concern, we encourage you to consult a moon phase calendar specific to your time zone.

Top 3 Goals

_____

_____

_____

Weekly Alignment

Focus

Habit Tracking

⬡ = _____

◯ = _____

☐ = _____

✦ = _____

Rituals For Thrivin

- EXERCISE
- MEDITATE / BREATHE
- JOURNAL
- DANCE
- GO ON A DATE
- CONNECT WITH NATURE
- VISUALIZE
- FAMILY TIME
- COOK / EAT A HEALTHY MEA
- ORGANIZE MY SPACE / LIFE
- GET RID OF THINGS I DON'T L
- BE WITH FRIENDS
- PLAY
- LET GO / FORGIVE
- SING / MAKE MUSIC
- CREATE ART
- READ FOR ENJOYMENT
- CONNECT / PRAY
- CALL SOMEONE / WRITE A LE
- STRETCH / DO YOGA
- MASSAGE / EXCHANGE TOUC
- SERVE MY COMMUNITY
- TECHNOLOGY BREAK

RITUALS FOR LIVING CHALLENGE

{ THIS WEEK, TURN UP THE VOLUME ON YOUR INNER PESSIMIST. DON'T LET NEGATIVE THOUGHTS RUN YOU FROM 'BELOW THE RADAR.' MAKE THE THOUGHTS "LOUD" ENOUGH TO HEAR THEM, THEN CHALLENGE THEM, LAUGH AT THEM, BREATHE INTO THEM, FORGIVE THEM. }

Wins from last week (what I gained / how I grew)

_____

_____

How will I reframe something I find difficult, painful, or stressful?

_____

_____

How will I create more freedom in my life this week?

_____

_____

Capture Your Brilliance - Dream, Expand, Record, Reflect:

Create your own dynamic balance.

- The Well Life Book

Tasks

- MONTHLY PLAN
- INCOMPLETE FROM LAST WEEK
- LIFE DUTIES
- ★ STAR THE MOST IMPORTANT TASKS

AUGUST 28, 2023	AUGUST 29, 2023	AUGUST 30, 2023
MONDAY	TUESDAY	WEDNESDAY ○
INTENTION:	INTENTION:	INTENTION:
:	:	:
:	:	:
:	:	:
:	:	:
:	:	:
:	:	:
:	:	:
:	:	:
:	:	:
:	:	:
:	:	:
:	:	:
:	:	:
:	:	:
WHAT SHALL I BE FOCUSED ON?	WHERE IS MY ATTENTION GOING?	WHAT PERSPECTIVE DO I CHOOSE?
:	:	:
:	:	:
:	:	:
:	:	:
:	:	:
:	:	:
:	:	:
:	:	:
:	:	:
:	:	:
:	:	:
:	:	:
:	:	:
I AM GRATEFUL FOR:	I AM GRATEFUL FOR:	I AM GRATEFUL FOR:

Final task: schedule next week!
NOW, PUT THESE TASKS & RITUALS
IN YOUR CALENDAR.
GO FORTH AND BE AWESOME!

AUGUST 31, 2023	SEPTEMBER 1, 2023	SEPTEMBER 2, 2023	SEPTEMBER 3, 2023
THURSDAY	FRIDAY	SATURDAY	SUNDAY
INTENTION:	INTENTION:	INTENTION:	INTENTION:
:	:	:	:
:	:	:	:
:	:	:	:
:	:	:	:
:	:	:	:
:	:	:	:
:	:	:	:
:	:	:	:
:	:	:	:
:	:	:	:
:	:	:	:
:	:	:	:
:	:	:	:
:	:	:	:
:	:	:	:
:	:	:	:
HOW AM I SPENDING MY ENERGY?	HOW DO I AFFECT MY WORLD?	WHAT COULD I LET GO OF?	WHAT IS WORKING WELL FOR ME?
:	:	:	:
:	:	:	:
:	:	:	:
:	:	:	:
:	:	:	:
:	:	:	:
:	:	:	:
:	:	:	:
:	:	:	:
:	:	:	:
:	:	:	:
:	:	:	:
I AM GRATEFUL FOR:	I AM GRATEFUL FOR:	I AM GRATEFUL FOR:	I AM GRATEFUL FOR:

Top 3 Goals

_____

_____

_____

Weekly Alignment

Focus

Rituals For Thriving

- o EXERCISE
- o MEDITATE / BREATHE
- o JOURNAL
- o DANCE
- o GO ON A DATE
- o CONNECT WITH NATURE
- o VISUALIZE
- o FAMILY TIME
- o COOK / EAT A HEALTHY MEAL
- o ORGANIZE MY SPACE / LIFE
- o GET RID OF THINGS I DON'T LO
- o BE WITH FRIENDS
- o PLAY
- o LET GO / FORGIVE
- o SING / MAKE MUSIC
- o CREATE ART
- o READ FOR ENJOYMENT
- o CONNECT / PRAY
- o CALL SOMEONE / WRITE A LE
- o STRETCH / DO YOGA
- o MASSAGE / EXCHANGE TOUCH
- o SERVE MY COMMUNITY
- o TECHNOLOGY BREAK

Habit Tracking

⬡ = _____

◯ = _____

▢ = _____

✦ = _____

RITUALS FOR LIVING CHALLENGE

{ LOOK AND LISTEN FOR GOOD SIGNS, BEAUTY, & FASCINATING THINGS. TALK ABOUT THEM, SHARE THEM, AMPLIFY THEM, SAVOR THEM. IMAGINE YOU TAPPED INTO A VEIN OF GOLD, AND NOW FOLLOW IT. JUMP FROM ONE GOOD THING TO THE NEXT. MAKE A GAME OF IT. }

Wins from last week (what I gained / how I grew)

_____

_____

How will I reframe something I find difficult, painful, or stressful?

_____

_____

_____

How will I create more freedom in my life this week?

_____

_____

Capture Your Brilliance - Dream, Expand, Record, Reflect:

Tasks

- MONTHLY PLAN
- INCOMPLETE FROM LAST WEEK
- LIFE DUTIES
- ★ STAR THE MOST IMPORTANT TASKS

SEPTEMBER 4, 2023	SEPTEMBER 5, 2023	SEPTEMBER 6, 2023
MONDAY	TUESDAY	WEDNESDAY ◐
INTENTION:	INTENTION:	INTENTION:
:	:	:
:	:	:
:	:	:
:	:	:
:	:	:
:	:	:
:	:	:
:	:	:
:	:	:
:	:	:
:	:	:
:	:	:
:	:	:
:	:	:
:	:	:
WHAT SHALL I BE FOCUSED ON?	WHERE IS MY ATTENTION GOING?	WHAT PERSPECTIVE DO I CHOOSE?
:	:	:
:	:	:
:	:	:
:	:	:
:	:	:
:	:	:
:	:	:
:	:	:
:	:	:
:	:	:
:	:	:
:	:	:
I AM GRATEFUL FOR:	I AM GRATEFUL FOR:	I AM GRATEFUL FOR:

Final task: schedule next week!
NOW, PUT THESE TASKS & RITUALS
IN YOUR CALENDAR.
GO FORTH AND BE AWESOME!

SEPTEMBER 7, 2023	SEPTEMBER 8, 2023	SEPTEMBER 9, 2023	SEPTEMBER 10, 2023
THURSDAY	FRIDAY	SATURDAY	SUNDAY
INTENTION:	INTENTION:	INTENTION:	INTENTION:
:	:	:	:
:	:	:	:
:	:	:	:
:	:	:	:
:	:	:	:
:	:	:	:
:	:	:	:
:	:	:	:
:	:	:	:
:	:	:	:
:	:	:	:
:	:	:	:
:	:	:	:
:	:	:	:
HOW AM I SPENDING MY ENERGY?	HOW DO I AFFECT MY WORLD?	WHAT COULD I LET GO OF?	WHAT IS WORKING WELL FOR ME?
:	:	:	:
:	:	:	:
:	:	:	:
:	:	:	:
:	:	:	:
:	:	:	:
:	:	:	:
:	:	:	:
:	:	:	:
:	:	:	:
:	:	:	:
I AM GRATEFUL FOR:	I AM GRATEFUL FOR:	I AM GRATEFUL FOR:	I AM GRATEFUL FOR:

Top 3 Goals

_____

_____

_____

Weekly Alignment

Focus

Habit Tracking

⬡ = _____

◯ = _____

▢ = _____

✦ = _____

Rituals For Thriving

- ○ EXERCISE
- ○ MEDITATE / BREATHE
- ○ JOURNAL
- ○ DANCE
- ○ GO ON A DATE
- ○ CONNECT WITH NATURE
- ○ VISUALIZE
- ○ FAMILY TIME
- ○ COOK / EAT A HEALTHY MEAL
- ○ ORGANIZE MY SPACE / LIFE
- ○ GET RID OF THINGS I DON'T LO
- ○ BE WITH FRIENDS
- ○ PLAY
- ○ LET GO / FORGIVE
- ○ SING / MAKE MUSIC
- ○ CREATE ART
- ○ READ FOR ENJOYMENT
- ○ CONNECT / PRAY
- ○ CALL SOMEONE / WRITE A LET
- ○ STRETCH / DO YOGA
- ○ MASSAGE / EXCHANGE TOUCH
- ○ SERVE MY COMMUNITY
- ○ TECHNOLOGY BREAK

RITUALS FOR LIVING CHALLENGE

{ THIS WEEK, TAKE A BREAK FROM STIMULANTS – COFFEE, CAFFEINATED TEA, YERBA MATE, ETC. IDEALLY SUGAR, TOO. DON'T LET THEM ROB YOUR ENERGY STORES OR MASK YOUR TRUE ENERGY LEVEL (AND KEEP YOU FROM ADDRESSING THE CAUSE, IF IT'S LOW). }

Wins from last week (what I gained / how I grew)

_____

_____

_____

How will I reframe something I find difficult, painful, or stressful?

_____

_____

_____

How will I create more freedom in my life this week?

_____

_____

Capture Your Brilliance - Dream, Expand, Record, Reflect:

Follow your words with actions that support them.

- The Well Life Book

Tasks

- MONTHLY PLAN
- INCOMPLETE FROM LAST WEEK
- LIFE DUTIES
- ★ STAR THE MOST IMPORTANT TASKS

SEPTEMBER 11, 2023	SEPTEMBER 12, 2023	SEPTEMBER 13, 2023
MONDAY	TUESDAY	WEDNESDAY
INTENTION:	INTENTION:	INTENTION:
:	:	:
:	:	:
:	:	:
:	:	:
:	:	:
:	:	:
:	:	:
:	:	:
:	:	:
:	:	:
:	:	:
:	:	:
:	:	:
:	:	:
:	:	:
WHAT SHALL I BE FOCUSED ON?	WHERE IS MY ATTENTION GOING?	WHAT PERSPECTIVE DO I CHOOSE?
:	:	:
:	:	:
:	:	:
:	:	:
:	:	:
:	:	:
:	:	:
:	:	:
:	:	:
:	:	:
:	:	:
:	:	:
I AM GRATEFUL FOR:	I AM GRATEFUL FOR:	I AM GRATEFUL FOR:

Final task: schedule next week!
NOW, PUT THESE TASKS & RITUALS
IN YOUR CALENDAR.
GO FORTH AND BE AWESOME!

SEPTEMBER 14, 2024	SEPTEMBER 15, 2023	SEPTEMBER 16, 2023	SEPTEMBER 17, 2023
THURSDAY ●	FRIDAY	SATURDAY	SUNDAY
INTENTION:	INTENTION:	INTENTION:	INTENTION:
:	:	:	:
:	:	:	:
:	:	:	:
:	:	:	:
:	:	:	:
:	:	:	:
:	:	:	:
:	:	:	:
:	:	:	:
:	:	:	:
:	:	:	:
:	:	:	:
:	:	:	:
:	:	:	:
:	:	:	:
:	:	:	
HOW AM I SPENDING MY ENERGY?	HOW DO I AFFECT MY WORLD?	WHAT COULD I LET GO OF?	WHAT IS WORKING WELL FOR ME?
:	:	:	:
:	:	:	:
:	:	:	:
:	:	:	:
:	:	:	:
:	:	:	:
:	:	:	:
:	:	:	:
:	:	:	:
:	:	:	:
:	:	:	:
:	:	:	:
:	:	:	:
I AM GRATEFUL FOR:	I AM GRATEFUL FOR:	I AM GRATEFUL FOR:	I AM GRATEFUL FOR:

Top 3 Goals

_____

_____

_____

Weekly Alignment

Focus

Rituals For Thriving

- ○ EXERCISE
- ○ MEDITATE / BREATHE
- ○ JOURNAL
- ○ DANCE
- ○ GO ON A DATE
- ○ CONNECT WITH NATURE
- ○ VISUALIZE
- ○ FAMILY TIME
- ○ COOK / EAT A HEALTHY MEAL
- ○ ORGANIZE MY SPACE / LIFE
- ○ GET RID OF THINGS I DON'T LO
- ○ BE WITH FRIENDS
- ○ PLAY
- ○ LET GO / FORGIVE
- ○ SING / MAKE MUSIC
- ○ CREATE ART
- ○ READ FOR ENJOYMENT
- ○ CONNECT / PRAY
- ○ CALL SOMEONE / WRITE A LET
- ○ STRETCH / DO YOGA
- ○ MASSAGE / EXCHANGE TOUCH
- ○ SERVE MY COMMUNITY
- ○ TECHNOLOGY BREAK

Habit Tracking

⬡ = _____

◯ = _____

▢ = _____

✧ = _____

RITUALS FOR LIVING CHALLENGE

{ THIS WEEK, PRETEND YOU ARE AN ENLIGHT-
ENED BEING. A SAGE. EMBODY THIS FULLY.
HOW DOES YOUR PATIENCE CHANGE? HOW
IS YOUR PERSPECTIVE DIFFERENT? HOW DO
YOU TREAT OTHERS DIFFERENTLY? HOW DO YOU
RESPOND TO HAVING YOUR BUTTONS PUSHED? }

Wins from last week (what I gained / how I grew)

_____

_____

How will I reframe something I find difficult, painful, or stressful?

_____

_____

How will I create more freedom in my life this week?

_____

_____

Capture Your Brilliance - Dream, Expand, Record, Reflect:

Tasks

- MONTHLY PLAN
- INCOMPLETE FROM LAST WEEK
- LIFE DUTIES
- ★ STAR THE MOST IMPORTANT TASKS

SEPTEMBER 18, 2023	SEPTEMBER 19, 2023	SEPTEMBER 20, 2023
MONDAY	TUESDAY	WEDNESDAY
INTENTION:	INTENTION:	INTENTION:
:	:	:
:	:	:
:	:	:
:	:	:
:	:	:
:	:	:
:	:	:
:	:	:
:	:	:
:	:	:
:	:	:
:	:	:
:	:	:
WHAT SHALL I BE FOCUSED ON?	WHERE IS MY ATTENTION GOING?	WHAT PERSPECTIVE DO I CHOOSE?
:	:	:
:	:	:
:	:	:
:	:	:
:	:	:
:	:	:
:	:	:
:	:	:
:	:	:
:	:	:
:	:	:
:	:	:
I AM GRATEFUL FOR:	I AM GRATEFUL FOR:	I AM GRATEFUL FOR:

Final task: schedule next week!
NOW, PUT THESE TASKS & RITUALS
IN YOUR CALENDAR.
GO FORTH AND BE AWESOME!

SEPTEMBER 21, 2023	SEPTEMBER 22, 2023	SEPTEMBER 23, 2021	SEPTEMBER 24, 2023
THURSDAY	FRIDAY ◑	SATURDAY	SUNDAY
INTENTION:	INTENTION:	INTENTION:	INTENTION:
:	:	:	:
:	:	:	:
:	:	:	:
:	:	:	:
:	:	:	:
:	:	:	:
:	:	:	:
:	:	:	:
:	:	:	:
:	:	:	:
:	:	:	:
:	:	:	:
:	:	:	:
:	:	:	:
:	:	:	:
HOW AM I SPENDING MY ENERGY?	HOW DO I AFFECT MY WORLD?	WHAT COULD I LET GO OF?	WHAT IS WORKING WELL FOR ME?
:	:	:	:
:	:	:	:
:	:	:	:
:	:	:	:
:	:	:	:
:	:	:	:
:	:	:	:
:	:	:	:
:	:	:	:
:	:	:	:
:	:	:	:
:	:	:	:
:	:	:	:
I AM GRATEFUL FOR:	I AM GRATEFUL FOR:	I AM GRATEFUL FOR:	I AM GRATEFUL FOR:

Top 3 Goals

Weekly Alignment

Focus

Rituals For Thriving

- EXERCISE
- MEDITATE / BREATHE
- JOURNAL
- DANCE
- GO ON A DATE
- CONNECT WITH NATURE
- VISUALIZE
- FAMILY TIME
- COOK / EAT A HEALTHY MEAL
- ORGANIZE MY SPACE / LIFE
- GET RID OF THINGS I DON'T LO
- BE WITH FRIENDS
- PLAY
- LET GO / FORGIVE
- SING / MAKE MUSIC
- CREATE ART
- READ FOR ENJOYMENT
- CONNECT / PRAY
- CALL SOMEONE / WRITE A LET
- STRETCH / DO YOGA
- MASSAGE / EXCHANGE TOUCH
- SERVE MY COMMUNITY
- TECHNOLOGY BREAK

Habit Tracking

⬡ = _____

◯ = _____

▢ = _____

✴ = _____

RITUALS FOR LIVING CHALLENGE

{ 3 TIMES THIS WEEK, BE A SOLAR PANEL. STAND IN THE SUN (IF IT'S ALWAYS BEHIND CLOUDS, THAT'S OK). FACE YOUR PALMS TOWARD IT AT CHEST LEVEL. IMAGINE YOU'RE ABSORBING SOLAR ENERGY THROUGH YOUR PALMS, STORING IT IN YOUR BODY, CHARGING YOUR BATTERIES. }

Wins from last week (what I gained / how I grew)

_____
_____
_____

How will I reframe something I find difficult, painful, or stressful?

_____
_____
_____

How will I create more freedom in my life this week?

_____
_____

Capture Your Brilliance - Dream, Expand, Record, Reflect:

The person who needs your forgiveness most is you.

- The Well Life Book

245

Tasks

- Monthly Plan
- Incomplete from Last Week
- Life Duties
- ★ Star the Most Important Tasks

SEPTEMBER 25, 2023	SEPTEMBER 26, 2023	SEPTEMBER 27, 2023
MONDAY	TUESDAY	WEDNESDAY
INTENTION:	INTENTION:	INTENTION:
:	:	:
:	:	:
:	:	:
:	:	:
:	:	:
:	:	:
:	:	:
:	:	:
:	:	:
:	:	:
:	:	:
:	:	:
:	:	:
:	:	:
WHAT SHALL I BE FOCUSED ON?	WHERE IS MY ATTENTION GOING?	WHAT PERSPECTIVE DO I CHOOSE?
:	:	:
:	:	:
:	:	:
:	:	:
:	:	:
:	:	:
:	:	:
:	:	:
:	:	:
:	:	:
:	:	:
:	:	:
:	:	:
I AM GRATEFUL FOR:	I AM GRATEFUL FOR:	I AM GRATEFUL FOR:

Final task: schedule next week!
NOW, PUT THESE TASKS & RITUALS IN YOUR CALENDAR.
GO FORTH AND BE AWESOME!

246

SEPTEMBER 28, 2023	SEPTEMBER 29, 2023	SEPTEMBER 30, 2023	OCTOBER 1, 2023
THURSDAY	FRIDAY ◯	SATURDAY	SUNDAY
INTENTION:	INTENTION:	INTENTION:	INTENTION:

HOW AM I SPENDING MY ENERGY?	HOW DO I AFFECT MY WORLD?	WHAT COULD I LET GO OF?	WHAT IS WORKING WELL FOR ME?

I AM GRATEFUL FOR:	I AM GRATEFUL FOR:	I AM GRATEFUL FOR:	I AM GRATEFUL FOR:

Life Edits

It's time to reflect on the past quarter, and decide what you want to refine as you move forward.

1. What was your biggest time and/or energy waster in the past quarter?

_____

2. Which activities and rituals yielded the biggest "return" for you (tangible or intangible) in the past quarter?

_____

_____

3. Review the habits you've been tracking in the last quarter. Reflect on the progress you've made and the habits you want to continue to work on as you move forward.

_____

_____

4. Is there anything you've been procrastinating over the past quarter?

_____

_____

5. What has been infringing on your happiness, health, or productivity in the past quarter that you intend to let go of in the coming quarter?

_____

_____

6. Self-Trust Personal Assessment: Compare your self-trust to the start of the year and see how you're doing. Rate your ability to trust yourself in each of the following areas of life on a scale of 0 to 10.

(Total lack of trust ⓪ ‥‥‥‥ ⑩ Complete trust)

COMMUNICATION: How much do you trust yourself to tell the truth, say what needs to be said for healthy relationships, speak kindly, & express yourself authentically? _____

DEPENDABILITY: How much do you trust yourself to show up for friends and family, and support them when they need it? _____

TIME MANAGEMENT: How much do you trust yourself to be on time, to stick to your schedule and to plan appropriately? _____

FOLLOW THROUGH: How much do you trust yourself to follow through on your projects, in the time frame intended, to completion? _____

FOCUS: How much do you trust yourself to stay focused on what you have chosen to work on & avoid indulging in distraction? _____

MONEY: How much do you trust yourself to stay conscious of what you have, to maintain a positive attitude around money & to avoid taking on unnecessary debt? _____

HEALTH MAINTENANCE: How much do you trust yourself to treat your body & soul well, to get the care you need & to be kind to yourself? _____

NUTRITION: How much do you trust yourself to make good food choices, to eat in a healthy manner & to stick with your agreements around eating? _____

WORK PERFORMANCE: How much do you trust yourself to honor the work you do, to do your best & to show up enthusiastically? _____

VALUES: How much do you trust yourself to live by your core values? _____

Quarter Four Breakdown

1. Get into your *ritual for planning* space. Do whatever you do to tune in (light a candle, take a breath, go to a peaceful spot, set an intention, etc.).

2. Look back at your What I Will Accomplish This Year list, and find all the projects that will be occurring in the coming quarter. Write each one in the table below and mark the appropriate month number(s) for the month(s) in which it will taking place.

Project	Month		
	Oct	Nov	Dec
	①	②	③
	①	②	③
	①	②	③
	①	②	③
	①	②	③
	①	②	③
	①	②	③
	①	②	③
	①	②	③
	①	②	③
	①	②	③
	①	②	③
	①	②	③
	①	②	③
	①	②	③
	①	②	③
	①	②	③
	①	②	③
	①	②	③
	①	②	③
	①	②	③
	①	②	③
	①	②	③

October
Project Breakdown

1. Get into your *ritual for planning* space.

2. Gather the projects from the Quarterly Breakdown that pertain to this month and write each one on a PROJECT line below.

3. Under the project name, enter all of the tasks that are involved in the project. Each of these tasks must be a single action step so that it can be put into your calendar and when you see it, no analysis needs to occur – you know exactly what to do.

_____
PROJECT

_____ _____

_____ _____

_____ _____

_____ _____

_____ _____

_____ _____

_____ _____

_____
PROJECT

_____ _____

_____ _____

_____ _____

_____ _____

_____ _____

_____ _____

PROJECT

_____   _____
_____   _____
_____   _____
_____   _____
_____   _____
_____   _____
_____   _____

PROJECT

_____   _____
_____   _____
_____   _____
_____   _____
_____   _____
_____   _____
_____   _____

PROJECT

_____   _____
_____   _____
_____   _____
_____   _____
_____   _____
_____   _____
_____   _____

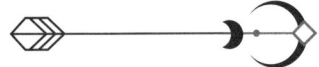

November
Project Breakdown

1. Get into your *ritual for planning* space.

2. Gather the projects from the Quarterly Breakdown that pertain to this month and write each one on a PROJECT line below.

3. Under the project name, enter all of the tasks that are involved in the project. Each of these tasks must be a single action step so that it can be put into your calendar and when you see it, no analysis needs to occur – you know exactly what to do.

_____

PROJECT

_____   _____

_____   _____

_____   _____

_____   _____

_____   _____

_____   _____

_____   _____

_____

PROJECT

_____   _____

_____   _____

_____   _____

_____   _____

_____   _____

_____   _____

_____   _____

PROJECT

PROJECT

PROJECT

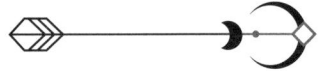 

December
Project Breakdown

1. Get into your *ritual for planning* space.

2. Gather the projects from the Quarterly Breakdown that pertain to this month and write each one on a PROJECT line below.

3. Under the project name, enter all of the tasks that are involved in the project. Each of these tasks must be a single action step so that it can be put into your calendar and when you see it, no analysis needs to occur – you know exactly what to do.

PROJECT

_____   _____

_____   _____

_____   _____

_____   _____

_____   _____

_____   _____

PROJECT

_____   _____

_____   _____

_____   _____

_____   _____

_____   _____

_____   _____

PROJECT

PROJECT

PROJECT

OCTOBER

Monday	Tuesday	Wednesday
(25)	(26)	(27)
2	3	4
9 Canadian Thanksgiving Indigenous People's Day	10	11
16	17	18
23 ♏ Scorpio 30	24 31 Halloween	25

Notes:

Thursday	Friday	Saturday	Sunday
(28)	(29)	(30)	1
5	6 ◐	7	8
12	13	14 ●	15 Navratri Begins
19	20	21 ◑	22
26	27 Mawlid al-Nabi	28 ○	29

●: New Moon ◐: First Quarter ○: Full Moon ◑: Third Quarter

ates for moon phases are based on the Eastern Time Zone of the United States. In other parts of the world these phases may technically ccur on the previous or following day. If precision is a concern, we encourage you to consult a moon phase calendar specific to your time zone.

Top 3 Goals

_____

_____

_____

Weekly Alignment

Focus

Habit Tracking

◯ = _____

◯ = _____

▢ = _____

✿ = _____

Rituals For Thriving

- EXERCISE
- MEDITATE / BREATHE
- JOURNAL
- DANCE
- GO ON A DATE
- CONNECT WITH NATURE
- VISUALIZE
- FAMILY TIME
- COOK / EAT A HEALTHY MEAL
- ORGANIZE MY SPACE / LIFE
- GET RID OF THINGS I DON'T LOVE
- BE WITH FRIENDS
- PLAY
- LET GO / FORGIVE
- SING / MAKE MUSIC
- CREATE ART
- READ FOR ENJOYMENT
- CONNECT / PRAY
- CALL SOMEONE / WRITE A LETTER
- STRETCH / DO YOGA
- MASSAGE / EXCHANGE TOUCH
- SERVE MY COMMUNITY
- TECHNOLOGY BREAK

RITUALS FOR LIVING CHALLENGE

{ THIS WEEK, CONNECT YOUR WHOLE BODY IN ALL YOUR MOVEMENTS. WHEN YOU STAND UP, SIT DOWN, WALK AROUND, WASH DISHES, TAKE A SHOWER, ETC, ENGAGE EVERY MUSCLE AND JOINT, INCLUDING YOUR ABDOMEN & BACK. BE GRACEFUL. DANCE THROUGH YOUR DAY. }

Wins from last week (what I gained / how I grew)

_____

_____

How will I reframe something I find difficult, painful, or stressful?

_____

_____

How will I create more freedom in my life this week?

_____

_____

Capture Your Brilliance - Dream, Expand, Record, Reflect:

Forgiveness isn't a single act, it's an ongoing commitment.
- The Well Life Book

Tasks

- MONTHLY PLAN
- INCOMPLETE FROM LAST WEEK
- LIFE DUTIES
- ★ STAR THE MOST IMPORTANT TASKS

OCTOBER 2, 2023	OCTOBER 3, 2023	OCTOBER 4, 2023
MONDAY	TUESDAY	WEDNESDAY
INTENTION:	INTENTION:	INTENTION:
:	:	:
:	:	:
:	:	:
:	:	:
:	:	:
:	:	:
:	:	:
:	:	:
:	:	:
:	:	:
:	:	:
:	:	:
:	:	:
:	:	:
WHAT SHALL I BE FOCUSED ON?	WHERE IS MY ATTENTION GOING?	WHAT PERSPECTIVE DO I CHOOSE
:	:	:
:	:	:
:	:	:
:	:	:
:	:	:
:	:	:
:	:	:
:	:	:
:	:	:
:	:	:
:	:	:
:	:	:
:	:	:
I AM GRATEFUL FOR:	I AM GRATEFUL FOR:	I AM GRATEFUL FOR

Final task: schedule next week!
NOW, PUT THESE TASKS & RITUALS
IN YOUR CALENDAR.
GO FORTH AND BE AWESOME!

OCTOBER 5, 2023	OCTOBER 6, 2023	OCTOBER 7, 2023	OCTOBER 8, 2023
THURSDAY	FRIDAY	SATURDAY	SUNDAY
INTENTION:	INTENTION:	INTENTION:	INTENTION:
:	:	:	:
:	:	:	:
:	:	:	:
:	:	:	:
:	:	:	:
:	:	:	:
:	:	:	:
:	:	:	:
:	:	:	:
:	:	:	:
:	:	:	:
:	:	:	:
:	:	:	:
:	:	:	:
:	:	:	:
HOW AM I SPENDING MY ENERGY?	HOW DO I AFFECT MY WORLD?	WHAT COULD I LET GO OF?	WHAT IS WORKING WELL FOR ME?
:	:	:	:
:	:	:	:
:	:	:	:
:	:	:	:
:	:	:	:
:	:	:	:
:	:	:	:
:	:	:	:
:	:	:	:
:	:	:	:
:	:	:	:
:	:	:	:
:	:	:	:
I AM GRATEFUL FOR:	I AM GRATEFUL FOR:	I AM GRATEFUL FOR:	I AM GRATEFUL FOR:

Top 3 Goals

Weekly Alignment

Focus

Habit Tracking

◯ = _____

◯ = _____

▢ = _____

✦ = _____

RITUALS FOR LIVING CHALLENGE

{ THIS WEEK, BE AN EMISSARY OF LOVE.
IMAGINE YOU HAVE LOVE BEAMING OUT OF
YOUR HEART, YOUR EYES, & YOUR VOICE, AND
THAT IT'S YOUR MISSION TO SHARE IT WITH THE
WORLD. EVERY INTERACTION – WITH PEOPLE,
ANIMALS, AND NATURE – IS AN OPPORTUNITY. }

Rituals For Thrivin

- ○ EXERCISE
- ○ MEDITATE / BREATHE
- ○ JOURNAL
- ○ DANCE
- ○ GO ON A DATE
- ○ CONNECT WITH NATURE
- ○ VISUALIZE
- ○ FAMILY TIME
- ○ COOK / EAT A HEALTHY MEAL
- ○ ORGANIZE MY SPACE / LIFE
- ○ GET RID OF THINGS I DON'T LC
- ○ BE WITH FRIENDS
- ○ PLAY
- ○ LET GO / FORGIVE
- ○ SING / MAKE MUSIC
- ○ CREATE ART
- ○ READ FOR ENJOYMENT
- ○ CONNECT / PRAY
- ○ CALL SOMEONE / WRITE A LET
- ○ STRETCH / DO YOGA
- ○ MASSAGE / EXCHANGE TOUCH
- ○ SERVE MY COMMUNITY
- ○ TECHNOLOGY BREAK

Wins from last week (what I gained / how I grew)

_____

_____

How will I reframe something I find difficult, painful, or stressful?

_____

_____

How will I create more freedom in my life this week?

_____

_____

Capture Your Brilliance - Dream, Expand, Record, Reflect:

Tasks

- MONTHLY PLAN
- INCOMPLETE FROM LAST WEEK
- LIFE DUTIES
- ★ STAR THE MOST IMPORTANT TASKS

OCTOBER 9, 2023	OCTOBER 10, 2023	OCTOBER 11, 2023
MONDAY	TUESDAY	WEDNESDAY
INTENTION:	INTENTION:	INTENTION:
:	:	:
:	:	:
:	:	:
:	:	:
:	:	:
:	:	:
:	:	:
:	:	:
:	:	:
:	:	:
:	:	:
:	:	:
:	:	:
:	:	:
:	:	:
WHAT SHALL I BE FOCUSED ON?	WHERE IS MY ATTENTION GOING?	WHAT PERSPECTIVE DO I CHOOSE
:	:	:
:	:	:
:	:	:
:	:	:
:	:	:
:	:	:
:	:	:
:	:	:
:	:	:
:	:	:
:	:	:
:	:	:
:	:	:
I AM GRATEFUL FOR:	I AM GRATEFUL FOR:	I AM GRATEFUL FOR:

Final task: schedule next week!
NOW, PUT THESE TASKS & RITUALS
IN YOUR CALENDAR.
GO FORTH AND BE AWESOME!

OCTOBER 12, 2023	OCTOBER 13, 2023	OCTOBER 14, 2023	OCTOBER 15, 2023
THURSDAY	FRIDAY	SATURDAY ●	SUNDAY
INTENTION:	INTENTION:	INTENTION:	INTENTION:
HOW AM I SPENDING MY ENERGY?	HOW DO I AFFECT MY WORLD?	WHAT COULD I LET GO OF?	WHAT IS WORKING WELL FOR ME?
I AM GRATEFUL FOR:	I AM GRATEFUL FOR:	I AM GRATEFUL FOR:	I AM GRATEFUL FOR:

Top 3 Goals

Weekly Alignment

Focus

Rituals For Thriving

o EXERCISE
o MEDITATE / BREATHE
o JOURNAL
o DANCE
o GO ON A DATE
o CONNECT WITH NATURE
o VISUALIZE
o FAMILY TIME
o COOK / EAT A HEALTHY MEAL
o ORGANIZE MY SPACE / LIFE
o GET RID OF THINGS I DON'T LOV
o BE WITH FRIENDS
o PLAY
o LET GO / FORGIVE
o SING / MAKE MUSIC
o CREATE ART
o READ FOR ENJOYMENT
o CONNECT / PRAY
o CALL SOMEONE / WRITE A LET
o STRETCH / DO YOGA
o MASSAGE / EXCHANGE TOUCH
o SERVE MY COMMUNITY
o TECHNOLOGY BREAK

Habit Tracking

⬡ = _____

◯ = _____

▢ = _____

✦ = _____

RITUALS FOR LIVING CHALLENGE

{ THIS WEEK, EAT SLOWLY. CHEW THOROUGHLY. PUT YOUR FOOD / FORK DOWN AFTER EVERY BITE. DON'T PUT ANYTHING INTO YOUR MOUTH UNTIL YOU HAVE SWALLOWED THE LAST BITE. BREATHE. SAVOR. STOP EATING BEFORE YOU FEEL FULL. }

Wins from last week (what I gained / how I grew)

_____
_____
_____

How will I reframe something I find difficult, painful, or stressful?

_____
_____
_____

How will I create more freedom in my life this week?

_____
_____

Capture Your Brilliance - Dream, Expand, Record, Reflect:

Free yourself from your limiting beliefs.
- The Well Life Book

267

Tasks

- MONTHLY PLAN
- INCOMPLETE FROM LAST WEEK
- LIFE DUTIES
- ★ STAR THE MOST IMPORTANT TASKS

OCTOBER 16, 2023	OCTOBER 17, 2023	OCTOBER 18, 2023
MONDAY	TUESDAY	WEDNESDAY
INTENTION:	INTENTION:	INTENTION:
:	:	:
:	:	:
:	:	:
:	:	:
:	:	:
:	:	:
:	:	:
:	:	:
:	:	:
:	:	:
:	:	:
:	:	:
:	:	:
:	:	:
:	:	:
WHAT SHALL I BE FOCUSED ON?	WHERE IS MY ATTENTION GOING?	WHAT PERSPECTIVE DO I CHOOSE?
:	:	:
:	:	:
:	:	:
:	:	:
:	:	:
:	:	:
:	:	:
:	:	:
:	:	:
:	:	:
:	:	:
:	:	:
:	:	:
I AM GRATEFUL FOR:	I AM GRATEFUL FOR:	I AM GRATEFUL FOR:

Final task: schedule next week!
NOW, PUT THESE TASKS & RITUALS
IN YOUR CALENDAR.
GO FORTH AND BE AWESOME!

OCTOBER 19, 2023	OCTOBER 20, 2023	OCTOBER 21, 2023	OCTOBER 22, 2023
THURSDAY	FRIDAY	SATURDAY	SUNDAY
INTENTION:	INTENTION:	INTENTION:	INTENTION:

:	:	:	:
:	:	:	:
:	:	:	:
:	:	:	:
:	:	:	:
:	:	:	:
:	:	:	:
:	:	:	:
:	:	:	:
:	:	:	:
:	:	:	:
:	:	:	:
:	:	:	:
:	:	:	:
:	:	:	:
:	:	:	:

HOW AM I SPENDING MY ENERGY?	HOW DO I AFFECT MY WORLD?	WHAT COULD I LET GO OF?	WHAT IS WORKING WELL FOR ME?
:	:	:	:
:	:	:	:
:	:	:	:
:	:	:	:
:	:	:	:
:	:	:	:
:	:	:	:
:	:	:	:
:	:	:	:
:	:	:	:
:	:	:	:
:	:	:	:

I AM GRATEFUL FOR:	I AM GRATEFUL FOR:	I AM GRATEFUL FOR:	I AM GRATEFUL FOR:

Top 3 Goals

_____

_____

_____

Weekly Alignment

Focus

Rituals For Thriving

- EXERCISE
- MEDITATE / BREATHE
- JOURNAL
- DANCE
- GO ON A DATE
- CONNECT WITH NATURE
- VISUALIZE
- FAMILY TIME
- COOK / EAT A HEALTHY MEAL
- ORGANIZE MY SPACE / LIFE
- GET RID OF THINGS I DON'T LO
- BE WITH FRIENDS
- PLAY
- LET GO / FORGIVE
- SING / MAKE MUSIC
- CREATE ART
- READ FOR ENJOYMENT
- CONNECT / PRAY
- CALL SOMEONE / WRITE A LET
- STRETCH / DO YOGA
- MASSAGE / EXCHANGE TOUCH
- SERVE MY COMMUNITY
- TECHNOLOGY BREAK

Habit Tracking

⬡ = _____

◯ = _____

☐ = _____

✿ = _____

RITUALS FOR LIVING CHALLENGE

{ THIS WEEK, COOK AT LEAST FOUR NICE MEALS. INFUSE THE FOOD WITH LOVE. IF YOU ALREADY COOK REGULARLY, CHALLENGE YOURSELF IN ANOTHER WAY – COOK SOMETHING REALLY SPECIAL, COOK A MEAL YOU'D USUALLY NOT COOK, OR COOK FOR SOMEONE ELSE. }

Wins from last week (what I gained / how I grew)

_____

_____

_____

How will I reframe something I find difficult, painful, or stressful?

_____

_____

_____

How will I create more freedom in my life this week?

_____

_____

Capture Your Brilliance - Dream, Expand, Record, Reflect:

Tasks

- MONTHLY PLAN
- INCOMPLETE FROM LAST WEEK
- LIFE DUTIES
- ★ STAR THE MOST IMPORTANT TASKS

OCTOBER 23, 2023	OCTOBER 24, 2023	OCTOBER 25, 2023
MONDAY	TUESDAY	WEDNESDAY
INTENTION:	INTENTION:	INTENTION:
:	:	:
:	:	:
:	:	:
:	:	:
:	:	:
:	:	:
:	:	:
:	:	:
:	:	:
:	:	:
:	:	:
:	:	:
:	:	:
:	:	:
WHAT SHALL I BE FOCUSED ON?	WHERE IS MY ATTENTION GOING?	WHAT PERSPECTIVE DO I CHOOSE?
:	:	:
:	:	:
:	:	:
:	:	:
:	:	:
:	:	:
:	:	:
:	:	:
:	:	:
:	:	:
:	:	:
:	:	:
I AM GRATEFUL FOR:	I AM GRATEFUL FOR:	I AM GRATEFUL FOR:

Final task: schedule next week!
NOW, PUT THESE TASKS & RITUALS
IN YOUR CALENDAR.
GO FORTH AND BE AWESOME!

OCTOBER 26, 2023	OCTOBER 27, 2023	OCTOBER 28, 2023	OCTOBER 29, 2023
THURSDAY	FRIDAY	SATURDAY ○	SUNDAY
INTENTION:	INTENTION:	INTENTION:	INTENTION:
HOW AM I SPENDING MY ENERGY?	HOW DO I AFFECT MY WORLD?	WHAT COULD I LET GO OF?	WHAT IS WORKING WELL FOR ME?
I AM GRATEFUL FOR:	I AM GRATEFUL FOR:	I AM GRATEFUL FOR:	I AM GRATEFUL FOR:

NOVEMBER

Monday	Tuesday	Wednesday
(30)	(31)	1
6	7	8
13 ●	14	15
20 ◐	21	22 ↗ Sagitarius
27 ○	28	29

Notes:

Thursday	Friday	Saturday	Sunday
2	3	4	5 Daylight Savings Ends ◑
9	10	11 Veterans Day	12 Diwali
16	17	18	19
23 US Thanksgiving	24	25	26
30	(1)	(2)	(3)

New Moon ◐: First Quarter ○: Full Moon ◑: Third Quarter

es for moon phases are based on the Eastern Time Zone of the United States. In other parts of the world these phases may technically r on the previous or following day. If precision is a concern, we encourage you to consult a moon phase calendar specific to your time zone.

Top 3 Goals

Weekly Alignment

Focus

Rituals For Thrivin

- EXERCISE
- MEDITATE / BREATHE
- JOURNAL
- DANCE
- GO ON A DATE
- CONNECT WITH NATURE
- VISUALIZE
- FAMILY TIME
- COOK / EAT A HEALTHY MEAL
- ORGANIZE MY SPACE / LIFE
- GET RID OF THINGS I DON'T LC
- BE WITH FRIENDS
- PLAY
- LET GO / FORGIVE
- SING / MAKE MUSIC
- CREATE ART
- READ FOR ENJOYMENT
- CONNECT / PRAY
- CALL SOMEONE / WRITE A LET
- STRETCH / DO YOGA
- MASSAGE / EXCHANGE TOUCH
- SERVE MY COMMUNITY
- TECHNOLOGY BREAK

Habit Tracking

⬡ = _____

◯ = _____

▢ = _____

✦ = _____

RITUALS FOR LIVING CHALLENGE

{ THIS WEEK, LIGHT A CANDLE AT ONE MEAL EACH DAY. LET IT REMIND YOU: TO PAUSE AND TUNE IN TO THIS MOMENT; TO INVITE MORE LIGHTNESS INTO YOUR LIFE; OF THE WARMTH AND UNIFYING POWER OF FIRE; OF MAGIC AND MYSTERY; OR OF A SPECIAL PRESENCE YOU'D LIKE TO INVITE TO THE MEAL. }

Wins from last week (what I gained / how I grew)

_____
_____
_____

How will I reframe something I find difficult, painful, or stressful?

_____
_____
_____

How will I create more freedom in my life this week?

_____
_____

Capture Your Brilliance - Dream, Expand, Record, Reflect:

Generate more positivity in the world.

- The Well Life Book

Tasks

- MONTHLY PLAN
- INCOMPLETE FROM LAST WEEK
- LIFE DUTIES
- ★ STAR THE MOST IMPORTANT TASKS

OCTOBER 30, 2023	OCTOBER 31, 2023	NOVEMBER 1, 2023
MONDAY	TUESDAY	WEDNESDAY
INTENTION:	INTENTION:	INTENTION:
:	:	:
:	:	:
:	:	:
:	:	:
:	:	:
:	:	:
:	:	:
:	:	:
:	:	:
:	:	:
:	:	:
:	:	:
:	:	:
:	:	:
:	:	:
:	:	:
WHAT SHALL I BE FOCUSED ON?	WHERE IS MY ATTENTION GOING?	WHAT PERSPECTIVE DO I CHOOSE?
:	:	:
:	:	:
:	:	:
:	:	:
:	:	:
:	:	:
:	:	:
:	:	:
:	:	:
:	:	:
:	:	:
:	:	:
I AM GRATEFUL FOR:	I AM GRATEFUL FOR:	I AM GRATEFUL FOR:

Final task: schedule next week!
NOW, PUT THESE TASKS & RITUALS
IN YOUR CALENDAR,
GO FORTH AND BE AWESOME!

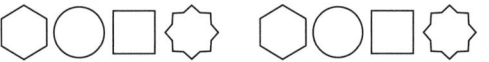

NOVEMBER 2, 2023	NOVEMBER 3, 2023	NOVEMBER 4, 2023	NOVEMBER 5, 2023
THURSDAY	FRIDAY	SATURDAY	SUNDAY ◑
INTENTION:	INTENTION:	INTENTION:	INTENTION:
:	:	:	:
:	:	:	:
:	:	:	:
:	:	:	:
:	:	:	:
:	:	:	:
:	:	:	:
:	:	:	:
:	:	:	:
:	:	:	:
:	:	:	:
:	:	:	:
:	:	:	:
:	:	:	:
:	:	:	:
HOW AM I SPENDING MY ENERGY?	HOW DO I AFFECT MY WORLD?	WHAT COULD I LET GO OF?	WHAT IS WORKING WELL FOR ME?
:	:	:	:
:	:	:	:
:	:	:	:
:	:	:	:
:	:	:	:
:	:	:	:
:	:	:	:
:	:	:	:
:	:	:	:
:	:	:	:
:	:	:	:
I AM GRATEFUL FOR:	I AM GRATEFUL FOR:	I AM GRATEFUL FOR:	I AM GRATEFUL FOR:

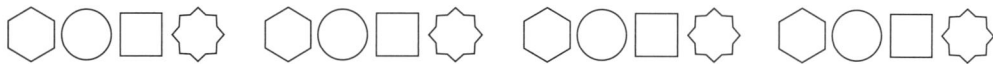

Top 3 Goals

_____

_____

_____

Weekly Alignment

Focus

Rituals For Thriving

- o EXERCISE
- o MEDITATE / BREATHE
- o JOURNAL
- o DANCE
- o GO ON A DATE
- o CONNECT WITH NATURE
- o VISUALIZE
- o FAMILY TIME
- o COOK / EAT A HEALTHY MEAL
- o ORGANIZE MY SPACE / LIFE
- o GET RID OF THINGS I DON'T LO
- o BE WITH FRIENDS
- o PLAY
- o LET GO / FORGIVE
- o SING / MAKE MUSIC
- o CREATE ART
- o READ FOR ENJOYMENT
- o CONNECT / PRAY
- o CALL SOMEONE / WRITE A LE
- o STRETCH / DO YOGA
- o MASSAGE / EXCHANGE TOUCH
- o SERVE MY COMMUNITY
- o TECHNOLOGY BREAK

Habit Tracking

⬡ = _____

◯ = _____

▢ = _____

⬡ = _____

RITUALS FOR LIVING CHALLENGE

{ THIS WEEK, EXERCISE TO THE POINT OF BREAKING A SWEAT AT LEAST 4 TIMES. IF YOU ARE EXHAUSTED OR HAVE BEEN CHRONICALLY ILL, INSTEAD USE THIS WEEK TO LEARN YOUR LIMITS. MOVE YOUR BODY DAILY, BUT NEVER TO THE POINT THAT IT LEAVES YOU MORE TIRED. }

Wins from last week (what I gained / how I grew)

_____

_____

_____

How will I reframe something I find difficult, painful, or stressful?

_____

_____

_____

How will I create more freedom in my life this week?

_____

_____

Capture Your Brilliance - Dream, Expand, Record, Reflect:

Tasks

- MONTHLY PLAN
- INCOMPLETE FROM LAST WEEK
- LIFE DUTIES
- ★ STAR THE MOST IMPORTANT TASKS

NOVEMBER 6, 2023	NOVEMBER 7, 2023	NOVEMBER 8, 2023
MONDAY	TUESDAY	WEDNESDAY
INTENTION:	INTENTION:	INTENTION:
:	:	:
:	:	:
:	:	:
:	:	:
:	:	:
:	:	:
:	:	:
:	:	:
:	:	:
:	:	:
:	:	:
:	:	:
:	:	:
:	:	:
:	:	:
WHAT SHALL I BE FOCUSED ON?	WHERE IS MY ATTENTION GOING?	WHAT PERSPECTIVE DO I CHOOSE
:	:	:
:	:	:
:	:	:
:	:	:
:	:	:
:	:	:
:	:	:
:	:	:
:	:	:
:	:	:
:	:	:
I AM GRATEFUL FOR:	I AM GRATEFUL FOR:	I AM GRATEFUL FOR:

Final task: schedule next week!
NOW, PUT THESE TASKS & RITUALS
IN YOUR CALENDAR.
GO FORTH AND BE AWESOME!

NOVEMBER 9, 2023	NOVEMBER 10, 2023	NOVEMBER 11, 2023	NOVEMBER 12, 2023
THURSDAY	FRIDAY	SATURDAY	SUNDAY
INTENTION:	INTENTION:	INTENTION:	INTENTION:
:	:	:	:
:	:	:	:
:	:	:	:
:	:	:	:
:	:	:	:
:	:	:	:
:	:	:	:
:	:	:	:
:	:	:	:
:	:	:	:
:	:	:	:
:	:	:	:
:	:	:	:
:	:	:	:
HOW AM I SPENDING MY ENERGY?	HOW DO I AFFECT MY WORLD?	WHAT COULD I LET GO OF?	WHAT IS WORKING WELL FOR ME?
:	:	:	:
:	:	:	:
:	:	:	:
:	:	:	:
:	:	:	:
:	:	:	:
:	:	:	:
:	:	:	:
:	:	:	:
:	:	:	:
:	:	:	:
:	:	:	:
I AM GRATEFUL FOR:	I AM GRATEFUL FOR:	I AM GRATEFUL FOR:	I AM GRATEFUL FOR:

Top 3 Goals

_____

_____

_____

Weekly Alignment

Focus

Rituals For Thriving

- EXERCISE
- MEDITATE / BREATHE
- JOURNAL
- DANCE
- GO ON A DATE
- CONNECT WITH NATURE
- VISUALIZE
- FAMILY TIME
- COOK / EAT A HEALTHY MEAL
- ORGANIZE MY SPACE / LIFE
- GET RID OF THINGS I DON'T LO
- BE WITH FRIENDS
- PLAY
- LET GO / FORGIVE
- SING / MAKE MUSIC
- CREATE ART
- READ FOR ENJOYMENT
- CONNECT / PRAY
- CALL SOMEONE / WRITE A LE
- STRETCH / DO YOGA
- MASSAGE / EXCHANGE TOUC
- SERVE MY COMMUNITY
- TECHNOLOGY BREAK

Habit Tracking

⬡ = _____

◯ = _____

▢ = _____

✦ = _____

RITUALS FOR LIVING CHALLENGE

{ THIS WEEK, AS OFTEN AS POSSIBLE, MAKE A CONSCIOUS DECISION TO FEEL LIGHT. LIGHTNESS IS ALWAYS AVAILABLE, EVEN WHEN THINGS SEEM DARK OR HEAVY. YOU CAN ALWAYS CHOOSE TO BE LIGHT. }

Wins from last week (what I gained / how I grew)

_____

_____

_____

How will I reframe something I find difficult, painful, or stressful?

_____

_____

_____

How will I create more freedom in my life this week?

_____

_____

Capture Your Brilliance - Dream, Expand, Record, Reflect:

Perceive and access your inner light.

- The Well Life Book

Tasks

- MONTHLY PLAN
- INCOMPLETE FROM LAST WEEK
- LIFE DUTIES
- ★ STAR THE MOST IMPORTANT TASKS

NOVEMBER 13, 2023	NOVEMBER 14, 2023	NOVEMBER 15, 2023
MONDAY ●	TUESDAY	WEDNESDAY
INTENTION:	INTENTION:	INTENTION:
:	:	:
:	:	:
:	:	:
:	:	:
:	:	:
:	:	:
:	:	:
:	:	:
:	:	:
:	:	:
:	:	:
:	:	:
:	:	:
:	:	:
:	:	:
WHAT SHALL I BE FOCUSED ON?	WHERE IS MY ATTENTION GOING?	WHAT PERSPECTIVE DO I CHOOSE
:	:	:
:	:	:
:	:	:
:	:	:
:	:	:
:	:	:
:	:	:
:	:	:
:	:	:
:	:	:
:	:	:
:	:	:
I AM GRATEFUL FOR:	I AM GRATEFUL FOR:	I AM GRATEFUL FOR

Final task: schedule next week!
NOW, PUT THESE TASKS & RITUALS
IN YOUR CALENDAR.
GO FORTH AND BE AWESOME!

NOVEMBER 16, 2023	NOVEMBER 17, 2023	NOVEMBER 18, 2023	NOVEMBER 19, 2023
THURSDAY	FRIDAY	SATURDAY	SUNDAY
INTENTION:	INTENTION:	INTENTION:	INTENTION:

HOW AM I SPENDING MY ENERGY?	HOW DO I AFFECT MY WORLD?	WHAT COULD I LET GO OF?	WHAT IS WORKING WELL FOR ME?
I AM GRATEFUL FOR:	I AM GRATEFUL FOR:	I AM GRATEFUL FOR:	I AM GRATEFUL FOR:

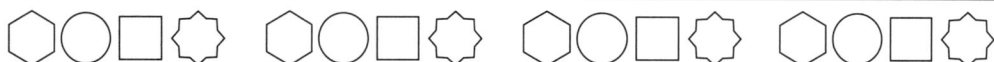

Top 3 Goals

_____

_____

_____

Weekly Alignment

Focus

Habit Tracking

⬡ = _____

◯ = _____

☐ = _____

✧ = _____

Rituals For Thrivin[g]

- ○ EXERCISE
- ○ MEDITATE / BREATHE
- ○ JOURNAL
- ○ DANCE
- ○ GO ON A DATE
- ○ CONNECT WITH NATURE
- ○ VISUALIZE
- ○ FAMILY TIME
- ○ COOK / EAT A HEALTHY MEA[L]
- ○ ORGANIZE MY SPACE / LIFE
- ○ GET RID OF THINGS I DON'T L[O]
- ○ BE WITH FRIENDS
- ○ PLAY
- ○ LET GO / FORGIVE
- ○ SING / MAKE MUSIC
- ○ CREATE ART
- ○ READ FOR ENJOYMENT
- ○ CONNECT / PRAY
- ○ CALL SOMEONE / WRITE A LE[TTER]
- ○ STRETCH / DO YOGA
- ○ MASSAGE / EXCHANGE TOUC[H]
- ○ SERVE MY COMMUNITY
- ○ TECHNOLOGY BREAK

RITUALS FOR LIVING CHALLENGE

{ THIS WEEK, ENGAGE IN SOME FORM OF PLAY – REAL PLAY, IN WHICH YOU IDEALLY ABANDON YOUR SELF-CONSCIOUSNESS AND LET LOOSE – ON AT LEAST FOUR DAYS. }

Wins from last week (what I gained / how I grew)

_____

_____

How will I reframe something I find difficult, painful, or stressful?

_____

_____

How will I create more freedom in my life this week?

_____

_____

Capture Your Brilliance - Dream, Expand, Record, Reflect:

Tasks

- MONTHLY PLAN
- INCOMPLETE FROM LAST WEEK
- LIFE DUTIES
- ★ STAR THE MOST IMPORTANT TASKS

NOVEMBER 20, 2023	NOVEMBER 21, 2023	NOVEMBER 22, 2023
MONDAY ◑	TUESDAY	WEDNESDAY
INTENTION:	INTENTION:	INTENTION:
:	:	:
:	:	:
:	:	:
:	:	:
:	:	:
:	:	:
:	:	:
:	:	:
:	:	:
:	:	:
:	:	:
:	:	:
:	:	:
:	:	:
:	:	:
WHAT SHALL I BE FOCUSED ON?	WHERE IS MY ATTENTION GOING?	WHAT PERSPECTIVE DO I CHOOSE?
:	:	:
:	:	:
:	:	:
:	:	:
:	:	:
:	:	:
:	:	:
:	:	:
:	:	:
:	:	:
:	:	:
:	:	:
I AM GRATEFUL FOR:	I AM GRATEFUL FOR:	I AM GRATEFUL FOR:

Final task: schedule next week!
NOW, PUT THESE TASKS & RITUALS
IN YOUR CALENDAR.
GO FORTH AND BE AWESOME!

NOVEMBER 23, 2023	NOVEMBER 24, 2023	NOVEMBER 25, 2023	NOVEMBER 26, 2023
THURSDAY	FRIDAY	SATURDAY	SUNDAY
INTENTION:	INTENTION:	INTENTION:	INTENTION:
:	:	:	:
:	:	:	:
:	:	:	:
:	:	:	:
:	:	:	:
:	:	:	:
:	:	:	:
:	:	:	:
:	:	:	:
:	:	:	:
:	:	:	:
:	:	:	:
:	:	:	:
:	:	:	:
:	:	:	:
HOW AM I SPENDING MY ENERGY?	HOW DO I AFFECT MY WORLD?	WHAT COULD I LET GO OF?	WHAT IS WORKING WELL FOR ME?
:	:	:	:
:	:	:	:
:	:	:	:
:	:	:	:
:	:	:	:
:	:	:	:
:	:	:	:
:	:	:	:
:	:	:	:
:	:	:	:
:	:	:	:
:	:	:	:
I AM GRATEFUL FOR:	I AM GRATEFUL FOR:	I AM GRATEFUL FOR:	I AM GRATEFUL FOR:

DECEMBER

Monday	Tuesday	Wednesday
(27)	(28)	(29)
4	5 ◐	6
11	12 ●	13
18	19 ◑	20
25 Christmas Day	26 Kwanzaa Begins Boxing Day (Can, UK) ○	27

Notes:

Thursday	Friday	Saturday	Sunday
(30)	1	2	3
7 Chanukah Begins	8	9	10 Human Rights Day
14	15	16	17
21 Winter Solstice	22 ♑ Capricorn	23	24 Christmas Eve
28	29	30	31 New Year's Eve

●: New Moon ◐: First Quarter ○: Full Moon ◑: Third Quarter

ates for moon phases are based on the Eastern Time Zone of the United States. In other parts of the world these phases may technically cur on the previous or following day. If precision is a concern, we encourage you to consult a moon phase calendar specific to your time zone.

Top 3 Goals

_____

_____

_____

Weekly Alignment

Focus

Habit Tracking

⬡ = _____

◯ = _____

▢ = _____

✦ = _____

RITUALS FOR LIVING CHALLENGE

{ THIS WEEK, EVERY TIME YOU WASH YOURSELF (HANDS, BODY, ETC.), SET AN INTENTION OF WASHING AWAY SOMETHING YOU'D LIKE TO LET GO OF THAT YOU'VE BEEN HOLDING ONTO, OR INTEND FOR THE WATER TO PURIFY OR NOURISH SOME PART OF YOURSELF. }

Rituals For Thriving

- EXERCISE
- MEDITATE / BREATHE
- JOURNAL
- DANCE
- GO ON A DATE
- CONNECT WITH NATURE
- VISUALIZE
- FAMILY TIME
- COOK / EAT A HEALTHY MEAL
- ORGANIZE MY SPACE / LIFE
- GET RID OF THINGS I DON'T LOV
- BE WITH FRIENDS
- PLAY
- LET GO / FORGIVE
- SING / MAKE MUSIC
- CREATE ART
- READ FOR ENJOYMENT
- CONNECT / PRAY
- CALL SOMEONE / WRITE A LETT
- STRETCH / DO YOGA
- MASSAGE / EXCHANGE TOUCH
- SERVE MY COMMUNITY
- TECHNOLOGY BREAK

Wins from last week (what I gained / how I grew)

_____

_____

_____

How will I reframe something I find difficult, painful, or stressful?

_____

_____

_____

How will I create more freedom in my life this week?

_____

_____

Capture Your Brilliance - Dream, Expand, Record, Reflect:

Expressing and receiving love connects you to a deep reservoir of energy.

- The Well Life Book

Tasks

- MONTHLY PLAN
- INCOMPLETE FROM LAST WEEK
- LIFE DUTIES
- ★ STAR THE MOST IMPORTANT TASKS

NOVEMBER 27, 2023	NOVEMBER 28, 2023	NOVEMBER 29, 202:
MONDAY ○	TUESDAY	WEDNESDAY
INTENTION:	INTENTION:	INTENTION:
:	:	:
:	:	:
:	:	:
:	:	:
:	:	:
:	:	:
:	:	:
:	:	:
:	:	:
:	:	:
:	:	:
:	:	:
:	:	:
:	:	:
:	:	:
WHAT SHALL I BE FOCUSED ON?	WHERE IS MY ATTENTION GOING?	WHAT PERSPECTIVE DO I CHOOS
:	:	:
:	:	:
:	:	:
:	:	:
:	:	:
:	:	:
:	:	:
:	:	:
:	:	:
:	:	:
:	:	:
:	:	:
:	:	:
I AM GRATEFUL FOR:	I AM GRATEFUL FOR:	I AM GRATEFUL FOR

Final task: schedule next week!
NOW, PUT THESE TASKS & RITUALS
IN YOUR CALENDAR.
GO FORTH AND BE AWESOME!

  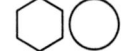 

NOVEMBER 30, 2023	DECEMBER 1, 2023	DECEMBER 2, 2023	DECEMBER 3, 2023
THURSDAY	FRIDAY	SATURDAY	SUNDAY
INTENTION:	INTENTION:	INTENTION:	INTENTION:
HOW AM I SPENDING MY ENERGY?	HOW DO I AFFECT MY WORLD?	WHAT COULD I LET GO OF?	WHAT IS WORKING WELL FOR ME?
I AM GRATEFUL FOR:	I AM GRATEFUL FOR:	I AM GRATEFUL FOR:	I AM GRATEFUL FOR:

Top 3 Goals

_____

_____

_____

Weekly Alignment

Focus

Habit Tracking

⬡ = _____

◯ = _____

▢ = _____

✷ = _____

RITUALS FOR LIVING CHALLENGE

{ TRY DRY SKIN BRUSHING AT LEAST 3 TIMES. GET A NATURAL SKIN BRUSH, UNDRESS, AND VIGOROUSLY BRUSH EVERY INCH OF YOUR SKIN, STROKING TOWARD YOUR HEART. START AT YOUR TOES AND WORK UP. THEN FINGERS TO HEART. THEN TORSO. (WWW.DREAMBOOK.VISION FOR MORE INFO) }

Rituals For Thriving

- EXERCISE
- MEDITATE / BREATHE
- JOURNAL
- DANCE
- GO ON A DATE
- CONNECT WITH NATURE
- VISUALIZE
- FAMILY TIME
- COOK / EAT A HEALTHY MEAL
- ORGANIZE MY SPACE / LIFE
- GET RID OF THINGS I DON'T LOVE
- BE WITH FRIENDS
- PLAY
- LET GO / FORGIVE
- SING / MAKE MUSIC
- CREATE ART
- READ FOR ENJOYMENT
- CONNECT / PRAY
- CALL SOMEONE / WRITE A LETTER
- STRETCH / DO YOGA
- MASSAGE / EXCHANGE TOUCH
- SERVE MY COMMUNITY
- TECHNOLOGY BREAK

Wins from last week (what I gained / how I grew)

_____

_____

_____

How will I reframe something I find difficult, painful, or stressful?

_____

_____

_____

How will I create more freedom in my life this week?

_____

_____

Capture Your Brilliance - Dream, Expand, Record, Reflect:

Tasks

- MONTHLY PLAN
- INCOMPLETE FROM LAST WEEK
- LIFE DUTIES
- ★ STAR THE MOST IMPORTANT TASKS

DECEMBER 4, 2023	DECEMBER 5, 2023	DECEMBER 6, 2023
MONDAY	TUESDAY ◑	WEDNESDAY
INTENTION:	INTENTION:	INTENTION:
:	:	:
:	:	:
:	:	:
:	:	:
:	:	:
:	:	:
:	:	:
:	:	:
:	:	:
:	:	:
:	:	:
:	:	:
:	:	:
:	:	:
WHAT SHALL I BE FOCUSED ON?	WHERE IS MY ATTENTION GOING?	WHAT PERSPECTIVE DO I CHOOS
:	:	:
:	:	:
:	:	:
:	:	:
:	:	:
:	:	:
:	:	:
:	:	:
:	:	:
:	:	:
:	:	:
:	:	:
:	:	:
I AM GRATEFUL FOR:	I AM GRATEFUL FOR:	I AM GRATEFUL FOR

Final task: schedule next week!
NOW, PUT THESE TASKS & RITUALS
IN YOUR CALENDAR.
GO FORTH AND BE AWESOME!

DECEMBER 7, 2023	DECEMBER 8, 2023	DECEMBER 9, 2023	DECEMBER 10, 2023
THURSDAY	FRIDAY	SATURDAY	SUNDAY
INTENTION:	INTENTION:	INTENTION:	INTENTION:
:	:	:	:
:	:	:	:
:	:	:	:
:	:	:	:
:	:	:	:
:	:	:	:
:	:	:	:
:	:	:	:
:	:	:	:
:	:	:	:
:	:	:	:
:	:	:	:
:	:	:	:
:	:	:	:
:	:	:	
HOW AM I SPENDING MY ENERGY?	HOW DO I AFFECT MY WORLD?	WHAT COULD I LET GO OF?	WHAT IS WORKING WELL FOR ME?
:	:	:	:
:	:	:	:
:	:	:	:
:	:	:	:
:	:	:	:
:	:	:	:
:	:	:	:
:	:	:	:
:	:	:	:
:	:	:	:
:	:	:	:
:	:	:	:
:	:	:	:
I AM GRATEFUL FOR:	I AM GRATEFUL FOR:	I AM GRATEFUL FOR:	I AM GRATEFUL FOR:

Top 3 Goals

_____

_____

_____

Weekly Alignment

Focus

Habit Tracking

⬡ = _____

◯ = _____

◻ = _____

⬡ = _____

Rituals For Thrivin

- EXERCISE
- MEDITATE / BREATHE
- JOURNAL
- DANCE
- GO ON A DATE
- CONNECT WITH NATURE
- VISUALIZE
- FAMILY TIME
- COOK / EAT A HEALTHY MEA
- ORGANIZE MY SPACE / LIFE
- GET RID OF THINGS I DON'T L
- BE WITH FRIENDS
- PLAY
- LET GO / FORGIVE
- SING / MAKE MUSIC
- CREATE ART
- READ FOR ENJOYMENT
- CONNECT / PRAY
- CALL SOMEONE / WRITE A LE
- STRETCH / DO YOGA
- MASSAGE / EXCHANGE TOUC
- SERVE MY COMMUNITY
- TECHNOLOGY BREAK

RITUALS FOR LIVING CHALLENGE

{ THIS WEEK, GET FLEXIBLE. STRETCH FOR AT LEAST TEN MINUTES EACH DAY. BREATHE INTO EACH PART AS YOU MEET RESISTANCE & ALLOW IT TO OPEN. MEANWHILE, STRETCH YOUR MIND. BE MORE FLEXIBLE AND OPEN WITH YOUR OPINIONS, BELIEFS, AND JUDGMENTS. }

Wins from last week (what I gained / how I grew)

_____

_____

_____

How will I reframe something I find difficult, painful, or stressful?

_____

_____

_____

How will I create more freedom in my life this week?

_____

_____

Capture Your Brilliance - Dream, Expand, Record, Reflect:

Love yourself deeply and completely.

- The Well Life Book

Tasks

- MONTHLY PLAN
- INCOMPLETE FROM LAST WEEK
- LIFE DUTIES
- ★ STAR THE MOST IMPORTANT TASKS

DECEMBER 11, 2023	DECEMBER 12, 2023	DECEMBER 13, 2023
MONDAY	TUESDAY ●	WEDNESDAY
INTENTION:	INTENTION:	INTENTION:
:	:	:
:	:	:
:	:	:
:	:	:
:	:	:
:	:	:
:	:	:
:	:	:
:	:	:
:	:	:
:	:	:
:	:	:
:	:	:
WHAT SHALL I BE FOCUSED ON?	WHERE IS MY ATTENTION GOING?	WHAT PERSPECTIVE DO I CHOOS
:	:	:
:	:	:
:	:	:
:	:	:
:	:	:
:	:	:
:	:	:
:	:	:
:	:	:
:	:	:
:	:	:
I AM GRATEFUL FOR:	I AM GRATEFUL FOR:	I AM GRATEFUL FOR

Final task: schedule next week!
NOW, PUT THESE TASKS & RITUALS
IN YOUR CALENDAR.
GO FORTH AND BE AWESOME!

304

DECEMBER 14, 2023	DECEMBER 15, 2023	DECEMBER 16, 2023	DECEMBER 17, 2023
THURSDAY	FRIDAY	SATURDAY	SUNDAY
INTENTION:	INTENTION:	INTENTION:	INTENTION:
HOW AM I SPENDING MY ENERGY?	HOW DO I AFFECT MY WORLD?	WHAT COULD I LET GO OF?	WHAT IS WORKING WELL FOR ME?
I AM GRATEFUL FOR:	I AM GRATEFUL FOR:	I AM GRATEFUL FOR:	I AM GRATEFUL FOR:

Top 3 Goals

_____

_____

_____

Weekly Alignment

Focus

Rituals For Thrivi[ng]

- ○ EXERCISE
- ○ MEDITATE / BREATHE
- ○ JOURNAL
- ○ DANCE
- ○ GO ON A DATE
- ○ CONNECT WITH NATURE
- ○ VISUALIZE
- ○ FAMILY TIME
- ○ COOK / EAT A HEALTHY MEA[L]
- ○ ORGANIZE MY SPACE / LIFE
- ○ GET RID OF THINGS I DON'T L[IKE]
- ○ BE WITH FRIENDS
- ○ PLAY
- ○ LET GO / FORGIVE
- ○ SING / MAKE MUSIC
- ○ CREATE ART
- ○ READ FOR ENJOYMENT
- ○ CONNECT / PRAY
- ○ CALL SOMEONE / WRITE A LE[TTER]
- ○ STRETCH / DO YOGA
- ○ MASSAGE / EXCHANGE TOUC[H]
- ○ SERVE MY COMMUNITY
- ○ TECHNOLOGY BREAK

Habit Tracking

⬡ = _____

◯ = _____

▢ = _____

✧ = _____

RITUALS FOR LIVING CHALLENGE

{ THIS WEEK, BE FASCINATED. NOTICE ALL THE TINY DETAILS AND INTRICACY. THE BRILLIANCE IN EVERY CREATION, BOTH NATURAL AND MANMADE. SEE THE PROFOUND BEAUTY AND DESIGN IN EVERY PEBBLE, EYE, OR PEN. TUNE IN, WAKE UP, BE FASCINATED. }

Wins from last week (what I gained / how I grew)

_____

_____

How will I reframe something I find difficult, painful, or stressful?

_____

_____

How will I create more freedom in my life this week?

_____

_____

Capture Your Brilliance - Dream, Expand, Record, Reflect:

Tasks

- MONTHLY PLAN
- INCOMPLETE FROM LAST WEEK
- LIFE DUTIES
- ★ STAR THE MOST IMPORTANT TASKS

DECEMBER 18, 2023	DECEMBER 19, 2023	DECEMBER 20, 2023
MONDAY	TUESDAY ◑	WEDNESDAY
INTENTION:	INTENTION:	INTENTION:
:	:	:
:	:	:
:	:	:
:	:	:
:	:	:
:	:	:
:	:	:
:	:	:
:	:	:
:	:	:
:	:	:
:	:	:
:	:	:
WHAT SHALL I BE FOCUSED ON?	WHERE IS MY ATTENTION GOING?	WHAT PERSPECTIVE DO I CHOOSE
:	:	:
:	:	:
:	:	:
:	:	:
:	:	:
:	:	:
:	:	:
:	:	:
:	:	:
:	:	:
:	:	:
I AM GRATEFUL FOR:	I AM GRATEFUL FOR:	I AM GRATEFUL FOR

Final task: schedule next week!
NOW, PUT THESE TASKS & RITUALS
IN YOUR CALENDAR.
GO FORTH AND BE AWESOME!

DECEMBER 21, 2023	DECEMBER 22, 2023	DECEMBER 23, 2023	DECEMBER 24, 2023
THURSDAY	FRIDAY	SATURDAY	SUNDAY
INTENTION:	INTENTION:	INTENTION:	INTENTION:
:	:	:	:
:	:	:	:
:	:	:	:
:	:	:	:
:	:	:	:
:	:	:	:
:	:	:	:
:	:	:	:
:	:	:	:
:	:	:	:
:	:	:	:
:	:	:	:
:	:	:	:
:	:	:	:
:	:	:	:
:	:	:	:
HOW AM I SPENDING MY ENERGY?	HOW DO I AFFECT MY WORLD?	WHAT COULD I LET GO OF?	WHAT IS WORKING WELL FOR ME?
:	:	:	:
:	:	:	:
.	.	.	.
:	:	:	:
:	:	:	:
:	:	:	:
:	:	:	:
:	:	:	:
:	:	:	:
:	:	:	:
:	:	:	:
:	:	:	:
:	:	:	:
I AM GRATEFUL FOR:	I AM GRATEFUL FOR:	I AM GRATEFUL FOR:	I AM GRATEFUL FOR:

Top 3 Goals

_____

_____

_____

Weekly Alignment

Focus

Rituals For Thriving

- ○ EXERCISE
- ○ MEDITATE / BREATHE
- ○ JOURNAL
- ○ DANCE
- ○ GO ON A DATE
- ○ CONNECT WITH NATURE
- ○ VISUALIZE
- ○ FAMILY TIME
- ○ COOK / EAT A HEALTHY MEAL
- ○ ORGANIZE MY SPACE / LIFE
- ○ GET RID OF THINGS I DON'T LC
- ○ BE WITH FRIENDS
- ○ PLAY
- ○ LET GO / FORGIVE
- ○ SING / MAKE MUSIC
- ○ CREATE ART
- ○ READ FOR ENJOYMENT
- ○ CONNECT / PRAY
- ○ CALL SOMEONE / WRITE A LET
- ○ STRETCH / DO YOGA
- ○ MASSAGE / EXCHANGE TOUCH
- ○ SERVE MY COMMUNITY
- ○ TECHNOLOGY BREAK

Habit Tracking

⬡ = _____

◯ = _____

☐ = _____

✦ = _____

RITUALS FOR LIVING CHALLENGE

{ THE WEEK OF EYE CONTACT: MAKE EYE CONTACT WITH EVERYONE YOU MEET. AS YOU DO, RELAX IN YOUR BODY. WHAT HAPPENS IF YOU MAKE A MENTAL COMMUNICATION WHILE HOLDING THEIR GAZE, SUCH AS, "I'M HERE FOR YOU" OR "I LOVE YOU"? SOUL WINDOWS. }

Wins from last week (what I gained / how I grew)

_____

_____

_____

How will I reframe something I find difficult, painful, or stressful?

_____

_____

_____

How will I create more freedom in my life this week?

_____

_____

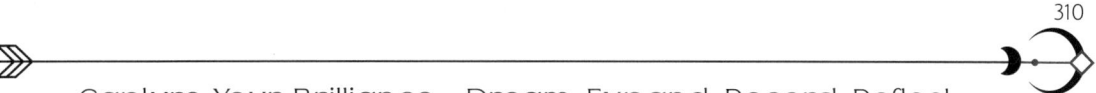

Capture Your Brilliance - Dream, Expand, Record, Reflect:

Make space in your life for the act of nourishing yourself. You are worth it.

- The Well Life Book

Tasks

- MONTHLY PLAN
- INCOMPLETE FROM LAST WEEK
- LIFE DUTIES
- ★ STAR THE MOST IMPORTANT TASKS

DECEMBER 25, 2023	DECEMBER 26, 2023	DECEMBER 27, 2023
MONDAY	TUESDAY ◯	WEDNESDAY
INTENTION:	INTENTION:	INTENTION:
:	:	:
:	:	:
:	:	:
:	:	:
:	:	:
:	:	:
:	:	:
:	:	:
:	:	:
:	:	:
:	:	:
:	:	:
:	:	:
:	:	:
:	:	:
WHAT SHALL I BE FOCUSED ON?	WHERE IS MY ATTENTION GOING?	WHAT PERSPECTIVE DO I CHOOSE
:	:	:
:	:	:
:	:	:
:	:	:
:	:	:
:	:	:
:	:	:
:	:	:
:	:	:
:	:	:
:	:	:
:	:	:
:	:	:
I AM GRATEFUL FOR:	I AM GRATEFUL FOR:	I AM GRATEFUL FOR:

Final task: schedule next week!
NOW, PUT THESE TASKS & RITUALS
IN YOUR CALENDAR,
GO FORTH AND BE AWESOME!

DECEMBER 28, 2023	DECEMBER 29, 2023	DECEMBER 30, 2023	DECEMBER 31, 2023
THURSDAY	FRIDAY	SATURDAY	SUNDAY
INTENTION:	INTENTION:	INTENTION:	INTENTION:
:	:	:	:
:	:	:	:
:	:	:	:
:	:	:	:
:	:	:	:
:	:	:	:
:	:	:	:
:	:	:	:
:	:	:	:
:	:	:	:
:	:	:	:
:	:	:	:
:	:	:	:
:	:	:	:
:	:	:	:
:	:	:	:
HOW AM I SPENDING MY ENERGY?	HOW DO I AFFECT MY WORLD?	WHAT COULD I LET GO OF?	WHAT IS WORKING WELL FOR ME?
:	:	:	:
:	:	:	:
.	'	.	:
:	:	:	:
:	:	:	:
:	:	:	:
:	:	:	:
:	:	:	:
:	:	:	:
:	:	:	:
:	:	:	:
:	:	:	:
:	:	:	:
I AM GRATEFUL FOR:	I AM GRATEFUL FOR:	I AM GRATEFUL FOR:	I AM GRATEFUL FOR:

 Reflect

Improvement is possible only through our capacity to reflect.

What were the most memorable moments of the past year?

_____

_____

_____

_____

_____

_____

_____

_____

What were your biggest challenges of the past year?

_____

_____

_____

_____

_____

_____

_____

How did you *ritualize* your goals, your health, and your happiness, and in what ways did this affect you?

_____

_____

_____

_____

_____

_____

_____

_____

What worked? What did you achieve over the past year?

_____
_____
_____
_____
_____
_____
_____

What didn't work? How might you do things differently in the future?

_____
_____
_____
_____
_____
_____
_____

What were the best lessons you learned?

_____
_____
_____
_____
_____
_____
_____

What was your theme for the past year? How did the year pan out with regard to this theme?

_____
_____
_____
_____

Someday Maybe List

Ideas that may or may not turn out to be worth pursuing.

 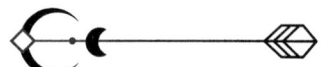

Items to Add to
Next Year's Plan

Ideas that are definitely worth pursuing.

_____

_____

_____

_____

_____

_____

_____

_____

_____

_____

_____

_____

_____

_____

_____

_____

_____

_____

_____

_____

_____

_____

_____

_____

_____

_____

_____

_____

_____

_____

_____

_____

_____

_____

_____

The most critical factor in planning effectively is doing it.

- The Well Life Book

Commitment is the continuous application of total participation.
- The Well Life Book

Difficulty is not a sign that you're on the wrong path.
- The Well Life Book

If you aspire to treat people well - with kindness, love, support, and patience - doesn't it make sense to start with the person closest to you? (We're talking about you.)

- The Well Life Book

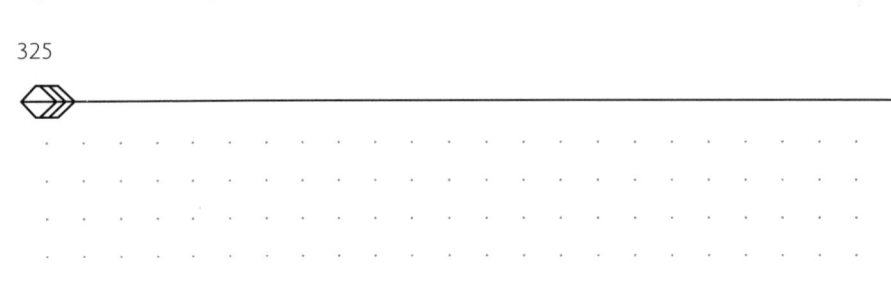

The light you're meant to follow emanates from inside you;
it's the light of your own virtue, illuminating the path in front of you.

- The Well Life Book

One of the best ways to empower an intention is to
let go of your resistance to not getting what you want.

- The Well Life Book

Love
You

For over a decade, our slogan has been "A peaceful world begins with a peaceful you."

Although peaceful individuals are the foundation of a peaceful world,

when it comes to initiating real change in a profound way,

we need people who are not just peaceful, but also powerful.

Individuals who have aligned their hearts with their ambitions.

Individuals who are dreaming and doing.

Individuals like you.

Thank you for making the world more awesome.

Love,

Briana & Peter